CW01494612

WILD WA_

WILD WALKS
Sixty Short North Island Walks

Mark Pickering

Photographs by Nic Bishop
& Mark Pickering

SHOAL BAY PRESS

Dedication

To Rachel for her enthusiasm and love

First published in 1996 by
Shoal Bay Press Ltd
Box 2151, Christchurch, New Zealand.

ISBN 0 908704 41 0

Cover photograph by Mark Pickering

Printed in Hong Kong through
Bookprint Consultants Ltd, Wellington
Distributed by Macmillan Publishers (NZ) Ltd,
6 Ride Way, Albany, Auckland. Fax (09) 415 6659

ACKNOWLEDGMENTS

Although I have visited all of these walks personally, I have gathered specific botanical and historical information from a wide variety of sources, including standard reference works, and *Forest and Bird* and *New Zealand Geographic* magazines.

In particular, I want to acknowledge the help of pamphlets (many of which are now out of print) that established a good background for my own notes. To these mostly unnamed writers in the old Forest Service, Lands and Survey Departments, and the newer Department of Conservation, I express my thanks. All errors are, of course, mine.

Several friends helped in the proofreading of the text, and made many helpful suggestions. I wish to thank Rachel Barker, Barbara Brown and Dave Glenny. Nic Bishop also supplied many of the excellent wildlife photos and Sven Brabyn helped with computer expertise.

In my peregrinations around the North Island I had the good fortune to be able to stay a night or two with friends, so I wish to thank Barbara Fountain and Laurence Dolan, Paula Kibblewhite and Bernie Kelly, Alan Hooker and Beverly Tatham, Kirsty Woods and Pete Williamson for their hospitality.

I also with to thank Noel Entwisle and Brits New Zealand for their generous assistance in lending me two campervans. It would not have been possible to write this book without their assistance and the campervans were comfortable and versatile.

Mark Pickering

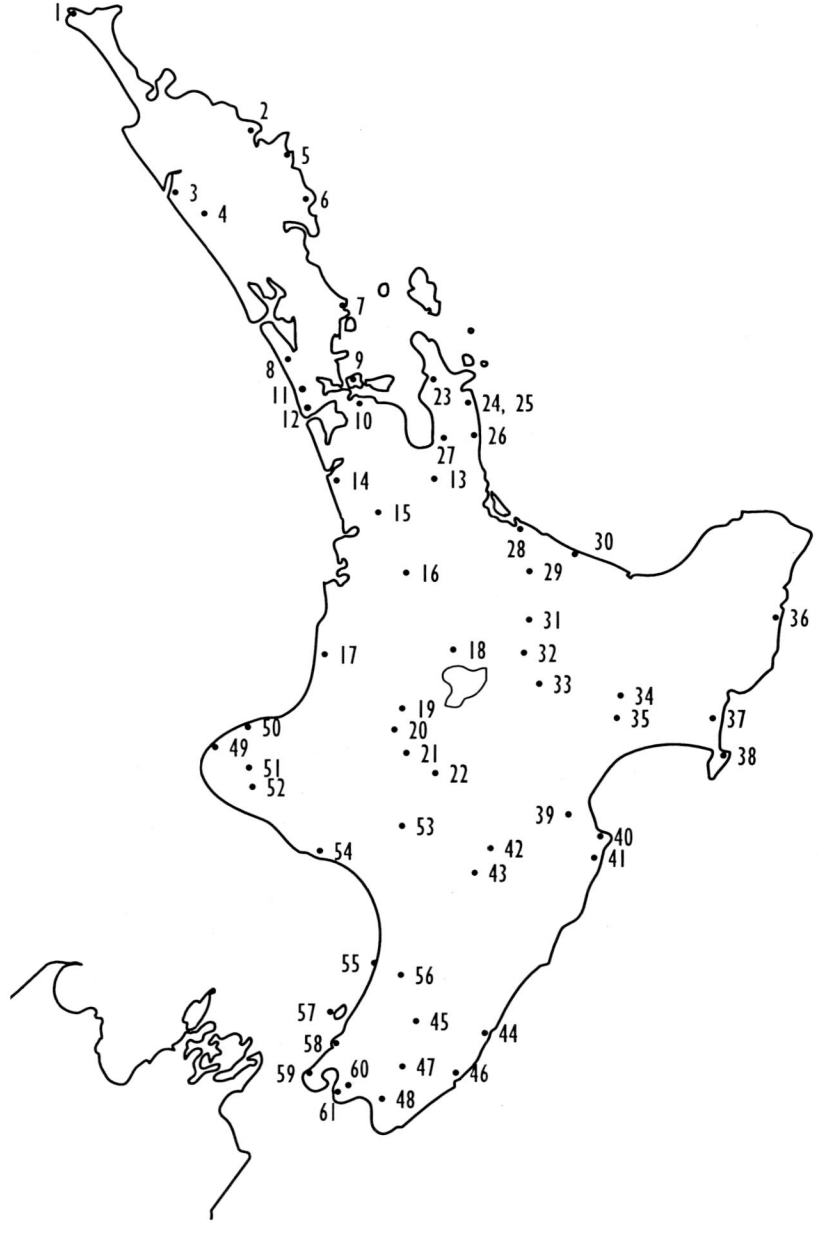

CONTENTS

INTRODUCTION

These outstanding short walks in the North Island will guide you into the ancient magic of wilderness. The walks selected each have a landscape feature or wildlife habitat that makes them unique. The 'wild' in the title refers to the quality of landscape, not the difficulty in getting there. For some people the idea is a contradiction: surely if you can walk safely and easily to these places they can't really be wild? Not so!

The North Island is blessed with wild places, and a good number of them are right under our noses. On a track like Paritutu Plug you can see gull rookeries, occasional fur seals and little blue penguins only 2km from the centre of New Plymouth. Similar wilderness experiences can be enjoyed close to many other urban areas, such as Tahuna-Torea Sandspit in the Auckland suburb of Glendowie, Ahuriri estuary right beside Napier, and Kohi Point overlooking Whakatane.

Some of these walks you can virtually *drive* to, such as The Plateau on Mount Taranaki and Manawatu estuary by Foxton Beach, but of course you miss the point if you stay in your car.

In many cases the best short walks are also the best for seeing New Zealand's wildlife and wild areas, and by combining walks and wildlife as a theme this book should appeal to a wide range of visitors to the North Island. The overseas do-it-yourself nature visitor, campervanners, and backpackers with independent transport will enjoy these walks, and even local people will be inspired to re-explore walks that they took for granted.

Features of the walks
- Each features some striking feature of landscape or wildlife
- Many types of habitat are represented: estuaries, rainforest, granite gorges, tussock plains, coastal lagoons, limestone outcrops, hot springs – the works!
- Anyone from grannies to grandchildren can tackle most of these walks. No special equipment is needed, apart from a parka and strong shoes.
- The walks are generally easy to get to and well-graded, with information signs and often toilet facilities.
- None of the walks takes more than four hours (return).
- The book contains a good geographical selection from around the North Island.

Things to take
Good footwear, strong shoes or light boots, a parka, some food and maybe spare warm clothes during the winter months. Keep an eye on the weather, and on coastal walks keep an eye on the tides.

Binoculars are a marvellous asset for wildlife spotting, and alleviate the stress on birds and animals when humans approach too closely for a 'better look'.

Best time to go

All year round is the obvious answer, but humans by and large prefer calm sunny days – naturally! Early morning and late evening are certainly rewarding times for spotting wildlife, and a region that may bustle with activity then, may by noon seem desolate. However, the more you come to study a particular area the more alive it seems; it's just a question of knowing where to look, and how.

Walking times

The walking times given here are conservative, and are designed to cater for slower walkers and families with younger children. Any adult of reasonable fitness can reduce these times considerably. Please tell someone where you are going, perhaps even leaving a written note.

Track information

A good number of these walks have information boards on site. Quite a few have had at one time or other pamphlets written describing the walks in detail, but many of these are now out of print. Most were produced by departments that are now extinct, such as the New Zealand Forest Service, or that now have no official interest in the area, such as the Department of Survey and Land Information (Dosli, formerly the Department of Lands and Survey).

But it is still worthwhile trying your local Department of Conservation office (DOC) which, even if it has not reprinted or revised the original pamphlet, may well have inherited some of the old stock.

There are several good field guide books for those interested in birds or plants. Both *Forest and Bird* magazine and *New Zealand Geographic* are highly recommended, with many in-depth articles on wildlife and wild areas.

For Lake Papaitonga, Geoff Park's book *Nga Uruora: the Groves of Life* is excellent, and for the Wairarapa's coastal geology there is Lloyd Homer and Phil Moore's *Reading the Rocks*. It would be inspiring if all geological books were as entertaining.

I also recommend the Andrew Crowe series of plants books *Which Native Fern?*, *Which Native Tree?* etc. They are a first-class introduction to the common New Zealand fauna.

Maps

The maps printed in this book are a simple visual guide to the area, and are not intended as a substitute for a topographical map. People who venture off the well-marked tracks should be equipped with detailed maps.

Guided wildlife tours

Throughout the North Island there are a number of commercial nature and wildlife tour operations. Some of these do not offer more than what an enterprising do-it-yourself wildlife watcher could see on their own account, although they can be convenient for people short of time.

However, some commercial operators have exclusive access to unique wildlife

10

that cannot be seen without joining their tour. Commercial arrangements between the Department of Conservation and the operators are designed to better control the management of a particular wildlife and reduce the stress on the animal or bird.

The text will mention if there is a commercial operation for a unique wildlife that cannot otherwise be easily seen. Some operations are seasonal, and may be closed if there is no wildlife activity, or if the wildlife is sensitive to disturbance.

Drinking the water

A water-borne parasite protozoa called giardia has become something of an issue in New Zealand in recent years, and has been identified in some freshwater streams throughout the country. It is an intestinal bug that causes diarrhoea and vomiting, and, in extreme cases, death. Fortunately it is easily cured and for most people is a nuisance rather than a threat.

Giardia has been in New Zealand for a long time, at least since the return of soldiers from both World Wars and it was possibly brought in by the early European settlers and the goldminers in the 1860s. Many Department of Conservation information boards in wilderness areas now carry warnings to travellers not to drink water from nearby streams. But although it has been called the traveller's disease, giardia actually occurs mostly in cities as a result of poor hygiene where contact with faeces is possible. Places such as kindergartens are particularly prone.

People should carry their own water if they are doubtful of the local stuff. Generally any water running through farmland should be treated with suspicion, and people should wash their hands carefully after going to the toilet. It is a pity to have to automatically distrust all freshwater creeks in wilderness areas, and this author has no intention of doing so. Recent scientific articles suggest that in order to absorb the 10 giardia cysts necessary to start an infection you need to drink something like 100 litres of water from a stream. Cheers!

Vandalism and graffiti

Because many of these walks are close to towns they periodically suffer from vandals wrecking signs, smashing glass, shooting wildlife etc. If you see the aftermath of any such behaviour please contact the local Department of Conservation office. If you actually *see* some vandals in action, or some suspicious behaviour, take down their number plate and report it.

Sadly, some areas have become prone to graffiti. It's true that in some historic areas, the Maori and European pioneers left similar personal graffiti, but since then we have multiplied alarmingly. While it is interesting if one or two early travellers made a mark, it is meaningless when hundreds do so.

Mountain bikes

Mountain bikes are generally not permitted on most of these tracks. Even where no specific prohibition exists, mountain bikers should look elsewhere, as tyre tracks can cause serious ruts, and a speeding mountain bike is incompatible with a walker on a gentle stroll.

Closure of walks
A number of these walks may be closed for certain times of the year. This is particularly true in rural areas during the lambing months of August to October. Other reasons for closure may be fire risk or wildlife management. Please respect these closures.

Wheelchair access
Some of these tracks are suitable for wheelchairs, but even on the best of them there can be obstacles such as bridges or tree roots that block progress. However, many of these walks start in visually interesting landscapes, which are rewarding in their own right, so people with disabilities need not feel they have to venture far to see spectacular places and unique wildlife.

TAKING CARE OF A WILD AREA
A few simple courtesies to the environment and to other users can keep these walks and their rightful inhabitants in their natural state.

Keep to tracks
Please keep to the marked tracks. This is particularly important in fragile wetland areas.

Keep wildlife disturbance to a minimum
Some wild creatures, such as harrier and weka, may seem to thrive on human presence, but this is not generally the case, and even the apparently successful birds mentioned suffer predation from dogs and shooting, or get accidentally poisoned.

No feeding
The Department of Conservation discourages people from feeding friendly birds such as wekas and keas, tempting though it is to do so. Particularly in the case of keas, it confirms them in their worst habits, disrupts their natural breeding cycles, and lures them away from their natural environment.

Injured wildlife
It is possible you will see injured wildlife, particularly birds. But remember that these birds are *wild*, and most have a nasty peck and may not take kindly to being 'rescued'. Wild creatures may not even *need* rescuing, but simply be resting, moulting, recovering from injuries, or quietly dying. If in doubt it is better to seek expert advice from the local Department of Conservation.

In the case of stranded whales or injured seals, the Department of Conservation should be contacted at once. DOC has built up a considerable amount of expertise in these situations and can provide experienced advice for members of the public who wish to help out. The public can play an important part in the rescue of the larger sea mammals.

No dogs

Nearly all these walks have significant and easily disturbed wildlife, and people often do not realise how damaging the presence of dogs can be. They may not necessarily kill any birds, or other wildlife, but continued disturbance, particularly at breeding times, can seriously interrupt breeding cycles, making it difficult for the birds to re-establish. Very often dog owners are themselves unaware of the consequences, and because they see no wildlife around mistakenly think it will be okay.

If members of the public see uncontrolled dogs in areas where they are inappropriate, they should be pro-active and take it upon themselves to remind the dog owners politely of their obligations. There are plenty of other public spaces for exercising dogs.

Some dog owners seem to regard the great outdoors as a huge dog toilet, and fouling is a persistent problem on many walking tracks these days, making it unpleasant for other users. Most councils have bylaws that require that you clean up after your dog so dog owners should ensure their pet has already been to the toilet in their own gardens, or else carry a pooper-scooper to remove the dog shit.

No fires

This is an obvious courtesy. Fires get out of control, disturb wildlife, and in the case of coastal forests the wood might not be as 'spare' or plentiful as it first seems. Rotting wood provides good sites for insects, which in turn provide the food base for geckos and birds. Take a thermos, and pre-cook your sausages.

No collecting

It is the most natural thing in the world to pick a flower or collect an interesting stone, but what do you do with the items when you get home? The flower wilts, and the stone gets put on a shelf above the toilet cistern and after a while chucked out into the garden.

Many of these walks are in fragile areas where if everyone grabbed a chunk of interesting material the consequences of degradation would be felt very quickly. People may think that 'their small bit' doesn't make a difference, but it does! Appreciate without possessing.

No shooting

Of course! Although many of these walks shelter animals that may be legitimately shot, such as rabbits or possums, the close proximity of walkers makes uncontrolled shooting dangerous and illegal. Noxious animal control in these fragile areas is best left to the council or government bodies, which can manage a controlled shoot at a minimal disturbance to existing wildlife.

No rubbish

Leave only footprints, take only photos. Carry out other people's rubbish as well.

WILDLIFE CODE OF CONDUCT

- If you see a wild creature keep a reasonable distance.
- If chicks or young animals are present, be especially discreet. Remember, the parents need be absent from their eggs in a nest only a few minutes to seriously affect the chances of those eggs hatching. And predators are always on the lookout for unattended young.
- Be patient.
- Approach slowly, avoid sudden movements or loud noises, and wherever possible reduce your profile.
- Do not come between the animal and their escape route (for example, seals and the sea).
- Do not feed animals.
- Get expert help for the 'rescue' of injured wildlife.
- Most birds and animals give warning signals or movements if they feel uncomfortable. Respect their space, and withdraw.

Food gathering

In the case of coastal areas where there is a vulnerable and unique habitat, the wildlife is usually more dependent on the food sources than you are. Shellfish beds can be depleted very quickly by humans, and people invariably take more than they really need. In many cases the coastal walks do not explicitly forbid gathering of shellfish, but it is certainly good behaviour to leave the food chain untouched.

Photography

All wildlife is vulnerable to disturbance at some point in its yearly cycle. Nesting birds, moulting penguins, seals with pups – all are particularly obvious and easy targets for a camera – but think of what the animal is feeling! A nest with the parents disturbed may be vulnerable to a predator, seals can be stampeded into the sea, and penguins are trapped by their moulting feathers and may damage themselves trying to escape.

Plenty of patience and skill is needed for good wildlife photography, and the chances are that unless you have a few days to spare, good lenses and a tripod, it is unlikely you will come away with any good ones – and you may have unnecessarily disturbed the wildlife into the bargain. The human eye is the best lens, along with a good pair of binoculars.

NORTHLAND

CAPE REINGA HEADLANDS

Features
Headland coast and views, swimming bays, Cape Reinga lighthouse, tidal platforms.

Cape Reinga there is a turn-off signposted Tapotupotu Bay, and it is a further 2km down to the bay.

How to Get There
From Kaitaia drive north almost 100km on a highway curiously named '1F'. Just before

Walking time
From Tapotupotu Bay to Cape Reinga 2 hours one way, 4 hours return.

Cape Reinga is the place where the spirit soars, literally and metaphysically. In Maori legend the souls of the dead take flight into immortality from the Cape, but a fair number of ordinary mortal souls are uplifted by the wild remoteness of this coast. Daunting beaches interrupted by headlands, mountainous sand dunes, rocky islets, passive lagoons, and a wind that keeps the coastal manuka from getting out of hand. The light is strong and the air uncluttered.

Some geography is in order. The long peninsula that juts out from Northland and starts approximately at Kaitaia township, is more formally known as the Aupori Peninsula. The Maori called it Te Hiku o te Ika (tail of the fish), and a glance at any map shows how appropriate this description is. The western side of this fish-tail peninsula is Ninety Mile Beach, while on the eastern side are three great estuaries: Rangaunu Harbour, Houhora Harbour and Parengarenga Harbour.

The top of the Aupori Peninsula is squared off and on the west side you have Cape Maria van Diemen with its photographable sand dunes, then Cape Reinga with its equally well photographed lighthouse. This is where all the tourist buses go, but it is not quite the northern-most point. Reinga has been translated as 'place of leaping'.

Spirits Bay occupies the middle of the squared-off peninsula and on the far east is North Cape, which is a scientific reserve and holds pride of place as New Zealand's actual northerly point. Sometimes people refer to the whole of the top of the Aupori Peninsula as Te Paki, which is the name of the farm (or station, in New Zealand

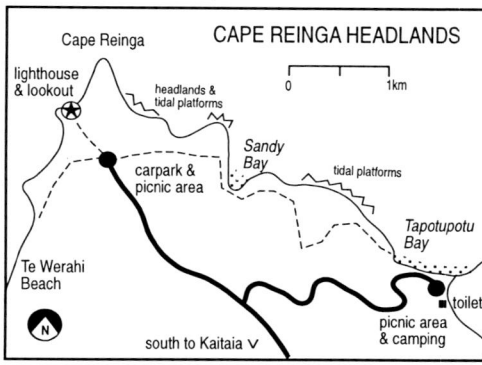

vernacular) that occupied all this land and was bought by the government in 1966. Te Paki is now a coastal farm park and has largely been opened up for public access, though it is still a working sheep and cattle station.

Ecologically, historically and scenically Te Paki is unique, and to explore all its virtues (and experience some of its weather vices) would take a week or so.

Northland green gecko

This short coastal walk gives you a good feeling for Te Paki's scenic theatre. The track starts at Tapotupotu Bay, which is a fine curve of sand trapped between two crisp headlands. The tidal platforms at the base of the cliffs are well worth exploring in their own right, as is the river with its sleek estuary exposed at low tide and the mangroves in the upper reaches.

Camping is allowed at Tapotupotu, and there are picnic tables and toilets, so that in the height of summer this place is more like a holiday camp than a remote wilderness. Fishing and diving are popular here. The coastal track is only a small part of a much longer network that starts at the far east of Spirits Bay and skirts around Cape Reinga to the top end of Ninety Mile Beach. Some walkers even go the length of walking Ninety Mile Beach, though you'd have to be bit mad.

From the west side of Tapotupotu Bay a modest grassy trail zig-zags up the headland, with occasional red marker posts. The views are good straight away and in places the track veers very close to the cliff edge. A thick Kenyan grass known as kikuyu abounds on either side of the track, and looks as if you can walk on it, but a couple of steps and you find yourself up to your knees in something that is more sponge than plant.

Most of the original kauri forest has gone from Te Paki and only remnants of broadleaf forest such as tarairi, puriri and kohekohe exist in the gullies. Flax is now common and manuka dominates, with its sweet-smelling flowers and leaves. North of Auckland the manuka is commonly known as kahikatoa.

Chaffinch and skylark are fairly noisy, as is the grey warbler. Every now and then the grass and manuka have slipped away to reveal gashes of bright red earth.

The track climbs to the top of the headland, then turns inland along an old vehicle

FLAX SNAILS

In the North Cape reserve there is a unique land snail found nowhere else in the world. Generally known somewhat inaccurately as the flax snail, the pupuharakeke actually prefers to live in the moist leaf litter under native trees such as tarairi, puriri and kohekohe. The snails were originally found on flax, probably because after the land clearance that was the only shelter available to them. They sleep by day and at night feed on leaves that have fallen to the ground.

In the hot, dry summer weeks some snails go into a dormant state and seal their shell aperture with dried mucus. A fully grown snail weighs about 17 grams. Grazing has reduced the plants that the snails prefer and opened up the canopy so that thrushes and blackbirds prey on the exposed juvenile snails.

There are three species of flax snail and North Cape is its stronghold, as are the Three Kings Islands. Maori inadvertently helped in the distribution of flax snails by taking them as passengers on the karaka trees they took with them to the Poor Knights Islands.

track before it cuts across the top of a gully onto another headland. You can see the Cape Reinga lighthouse now, as the track descends into a lovely bay given the rather prosaic name of Sandy. The Maori called it Ngatangawhiti Bay. This cove is pretty and secluded, with shady pohutukawa and more rock platforms to explore. A good place for lunch or a siesta.

It's a steep climb up the open spur to the lighthouse, but again the views are superb. At the carpark the world is suddenly crawling with people.

The distant sand dunes of Cape Maria van Diemen look stunning, and there's a tempting track down the other side of the carpark to Te Werahi Beach. But you have to look at the lighthouse, and take a photo or two. The interesting rocks immediately below the lighthouse are out of bounds because they harbour a host of nesting and roosting sea birds.

Once the Maori soul had slipped down the pohutukawa tree to the underworld it climbed up to one of the Three Kings Islands, which can be seen offshore, and here left finally for the world of its ancestors.

You might have arranged a car to pick you up here, otherwise at some stage you will leave the hustle and bustle of Cape Reinga and return the way you came, back along the headlands. From this direction it is like a different track, it really is.

WAITANGI MANGROVES

Features
Mangrove forest, Haruru Falls, historic site, estuary.

How to get there
Paihia in the Bay of Islands is about 60km north of Whangarei on Highway 1, turning off at Kawakawa. The Treaty House at Waitangi is 1km north of Paihia, and the east end of the mangrove walk starts by the golf course. For Haruru Falls take the Puketona road 3km and follow the signs to the carpark.

Walking time
2-3 hours one way, 3-4 hours return.

While some of the Northland coast is composed of romantic islands and great beaches , the rest of it is eaten away with mangrove backwaters, estuaries, and saltwater inlets. This has often been a shunned landscape, and much of it is only glimpsed from the roadside, so this walk is an excellent way to experience the private life of an estuary.

The boardwalk is probably about the best mangrove walk there is, and there are the added attractions of Haruru Falls and

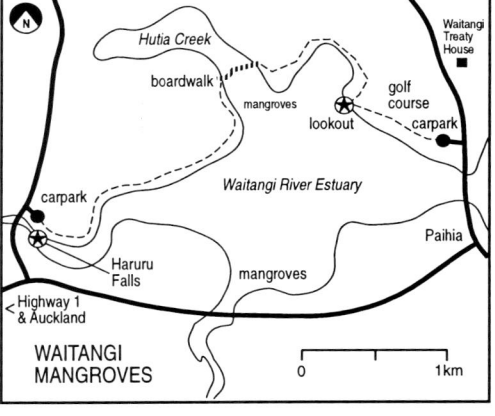

the coastal forest. At the small Haruru Falls carpark it is worth diverting to enjoy this wide, attractive falls. Haruru has been translated as 'roar' or 'thunder'.

The mangrove track follows the estuarine coast in a forest mostly composed of tree ferns, with kanuka, mapou and rangiora. Rangiora has the largest leaves, soft and white underneath, so it is easy to identify. Birds include the tui, bellbird, fantail, blackbird and grey warbler, with its parasite the shining cuckoo. Although this is only second-growth forest it is kiwi habitat, which might be heard if you make a night visit to the carpark.

It's an easy-walking forest trail that takes about an hour to get to the Hutia Creek inlet. The 250 metre boardwalk zig-zags through a swathe of mangroves, with information panels at appropriate sites.

The estuary looks empty yet is an abundance of life. Whelks, mud crabs (their small holes are everywhere), cockles, prawns, spire snails, barnacles and mudflat topshells are only a portion of the inhabitants. Neptune's necklace seaweed gets attached to the mangroves' air-breathing roots, which stick up like slimy fingers. The peculiar 'pistol popping' sounds are caused by the snapping shrimp, with has a grossly enlarged special joint for this (not clearly understood) purpose.

19

Estuaries are nurseries for many fish and over 30 species have been identified here. Yellow-eyed mullet, flounder, parore and eels are common, and at high tide big fish such as snapper, trevalli and kingfish have been seen.

The boardwalks and bridge are good places from which to see white-faced herons, though if you get too close they will fly off. Despite their elegant manner they have a coarse and throaty call. Shags are common, including little black shag, black shag and pied shag, and so is the bright sound and flight of the New Zealand kingfisher.

If you don't have transport at the other end, the footbridge is a good place to turn back. The coastal forest from here on gets thinner and more scrappy, though after 30 minutes you come out to a good lookout platform from which you can see the whole Waitangi estuary. Well worth it.

The track continues to skirt farmland and then a golf course, and it eventually pops on to a fairway just before the carpark. It's only about a 10-minute walk to the Waitangi Treaty House, which bustles with visitors and ceremony and seems oddly in contrast to the privacy of the estuary.

MANGROVES

Mangroves are unique and, until recently, unloved. Estuaries have never been a favourite habitat for urban humans, who are often turned off by the smelly mud, 'brown' views and 'useless land'. Mangroves compound this bad image. They impede access to the sea, have alien-like roots and make disconcerting sucking and popping sounds. However these 'sea forests' are winning defenders and admirers as their role is better understood.

NIC BISHOP

The mangrove is the only tree to grow in tidal waters, and has special adaptations to enable it to do so. Mangroves can secrete salt through their leaf surfaces, and their seeds germinate before leaving the parent tree. The distinctive aerial-breathing root systems ('snorkels'!) are crucial to their success, and the mangrove also forms 'root rafts', which stabilise it against tidal action, also stabilising the soil. The mangrove's sweet-smelling flowers attract bees, which make a distinctive fruity honey from them.

The mangrove is frost-tender and does not grow further south than Raglan or Opotiki, and it prefers sheltered inlets. However, it is suspected that mangroves could grow effectively further south, and indeed two plants were found in the South Island, in Parapara inlet in Golden Bay. Traditionally despised, mangroves form a unique coastal safety zone and trap silt between their roots which leads to natural reclamation. In time, a mangrove forest will do itself out of its own home, and humans scarcely need to busily remove them in order to 'improve' the coast.

Features
Coastal and harbour views, headland walk, reef platforms, beaches.

How to get there
From Opononi (Highway 12) drive south for 5km, then turn down Signal Hill Road and drive 2km to the well-situated carpark.

Walking time
1-2 hours on headland and beach, 3-4 hours return to Waiwhatawhata Stream beach. Low tide or mid-tide is definitely the best time.

Most evenings there's a fisherman or two on the reef platforms below South Head, tirelessly heaving out their lines and reeling them in, their upright stances silhouetted against the huge sand dunes on the other side of the harbour. Fishing trawlers chug wearily over the bar into Hokianga Harbour and somebody might be bending for kina in the rock pools. More successfully, white-faced herons will be picking over the high-tide deposits, and keeping a wary eye on the humans. Sometimes the fishermen get a fish, sometimes it's seaweed – nearly always there's a memory of twilight and salt to take back to the darkening towns.

Some places have more ambience than substance. The actual South Head walk you can knock off in five minutes, and down to the beach is about 10 minutes return. But it's a powerful piece of landscape, the sort of place that tends to get better the second or third time, and gets under your skin.

South Head is at the top end of the Waipoua Coastal track, Arai te Utu, a mammoth two- or three-day tramping affair that travels past the Waipoua kauri forest, then over Maunganui Bluff to the Kai Iwi Lakes. This walk only goes to the Waiwhatawhata Stream beach and back – a lot shorter but satisfying nevertheless. The carpark has a good view, but the short walking track to the old signal site is even better. The huge sand dunes on the North Head of Hokianga are awesome.

A benched track goes down to the beach, and you can spend an hour pottering among the extensive reef platforms that go to South Head. Large saucer-shaped pools

South Head, looking towards North Head

get left behind on the conglomerate rocks, some of them drenched with seaweed, and brilliantine sandy channels dissect the platforms at low tide.

South from the beach a large, surging sea cavern stops you fossicking much further, so it's back to the track, which climbs up through the jointed rush onto the breezy grass headland. A ring of encircling cliffs prevents access down to a secretive cove around the first shoulder, and the headland trail closely follows the cliff edge and fence-line. Skylarks are usually giving their all.

On a clear day you can see Maunganui Bluff way down south, before the track cuts through dune country onto a broad basking beach by the Waiwhatawhata stream. There are more tidal platforms at the north end, and a popular set of roosting rocks where shags congregate in erudite committees. You can gain a few lifestyle tips from the black-backed gulls that simply saunter along the surf line, and indeed seem to be rather good at it – South Head is that sort of place.

WAIPOUA KAURI FOREST

Features
New Zealand's two largest kauri trees, mature kauri forest, bush birds.

How to get there
Waipoua Forest is on Highway 12, about 30km south of Opononi and 60km north of Dargaville.

Walking time
Tane Mahuta is 10 minutes return, Four Sisters 5 minutes return, Te Matua Ngahere 30 minutes return.

'There were giants on the earth in those days' is how the Old Testament put it, and although the biblical writers were not thinking of the kauri at Waipoua, the metaphor seems apt. When you consider that these huge trees were part of the era of the great moas and the giant eagle, then the pre-human history of New Zealand was cluttered with giants. They are now mostly gone. These great kauri are the last of their kind and infinitely precious, and we are the underlings that brought them to their knees.

Most kauri has been logged and regions like Coromandel and Great Barrier are, as one writer bluntly put it, examples of 'the arboreal equivalent of genocide'. The remnant bits and

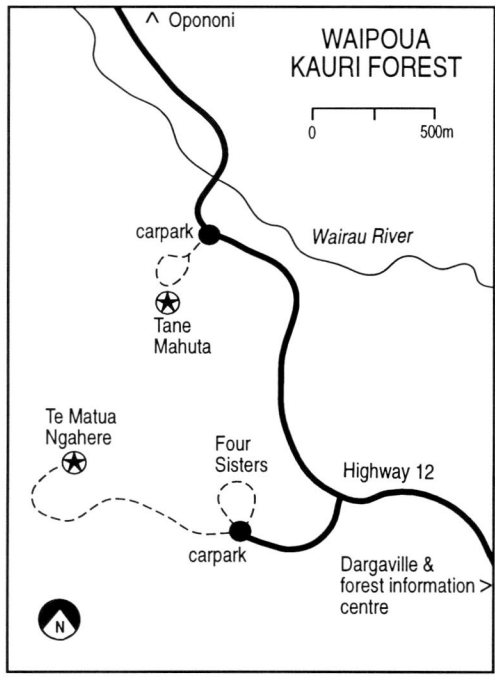

pieces remain though nostalgia, carelessness, or the dedicated activity of conservationists. Waipoua is the best kauri forest remaining, but is a tiny sanctuary really – only 2600 hectares of mature kauri, 9100 hectares of forest in total, and only finally preserved as late as 1952 after a prolonged conservation battle.

The drive through Waipoua is distinctly scenic in its own right, and twists about numerous large kauri trees – which for once have right of way. There's an information centre and motor camp at the forest headquarters, which is incongruously surrounded by pine trees. The forest lookout is worth a side-trip.

These three short walks can be done in an hour or so, but there are other, longer walks in Waipoua.

Tane Mahuta – 'God of the Forest'

The largest kauri ever recorded had a 23-metre girth and soared 21.8 to the first limb. Tane Mahuta is a bit of a stripling in comparison, with a mere 14-metre girth and 17 metres to the first branch. However, it is an awesome sight, as the track winds through lesser trees of tarairi and rimu and suddenly you are confronted with a solid wooden battlement of a tree, 1200 years old and topped with crenellated branches. There is enough wood in this tree to build 12 three-bedroomed houses – shudder the thought.

KAURI

Kauri is a conifer, a cone-bearing tree, with many unusual features. It starts life as a 'normal' looking tree in a nursery forest such as manuka. It grows through a teenage or 'ricker' stage, then abruptly thickens, and this middle-age spread swells into a vast cylinder while the crown becomes thin. Despite their enormous bulk, kauri are shallow-rooted and prone to wind-throw. The leaves are thick and leathery, unusually for a conifer, and the bark flakes off in dinner-plate-size chunks, which stops epiphytes from establishing a hold. Under mature kauri you find dense kauri grass, home to the good-looking kauri snail, a carnivore that feeds on earthworms and other insects. Kauri will live for up to two thousand years.

NIC BISHOP

Kauri bark

The wood is straight, clean, durable and gorgeous to look at, and it became highly prized last century. It was used extensively for ship-building and house-building in the colonial era. Kauri gum is a sticky white resin that is a natural 'plaster' and stops rot and infection from entering a tree wound. Professional 'gum bleeders' took advantage of this mechanism and bled the trees artificially, using their equivalent of a mountaineer's ice-axe and crampons to climb the tree. Kauri gum was originally used for varnishes, French polish and linoleum, but these days re-cycled kauri is reserved for specialist furniture and instrument makers. Maori used kauri gum torches and gum smoke as insect repellent. Mixed with the milk of puha, the gum made a sort of aromatic chewing gum.

The Four Sisters

An elegant boardwalk swings around four kauri growing cheek-by-jowl, and the boardwalk has been deliberately raised to protect the sensitive feeding roots. These and the associated humus from centuries of bark-shedding form a mound around the base of the trunk called pukahukahu. Parts of the now-sealed road through Waipoua have also been raised to prevent damage to the shallow root area of the kauri.

Te Matua Ngahere – 'Father of the Forest'

This is a profoundly impressive walk and perhaps the best of the three. You have time to immerse yourself in a mature kauri forest, and you pass by tree after massive tree on the way to the second-largest kauri in existence. There's a solid stillness in the air and you can see why people imagine they are in a botanical cathedral.

Mosses and ferns fill every niche on the ground, and epiphytes such as nei nei or *Dracophyllum* dangle off the trunks. On some kauri as many as 30 different species of epiphytes have been found – a perching forest within a forest.

Birds among the groves of kauri include tui, bellbirds, fantails, shining cuckoos, wood pigeons, grey warblers, tomtits, brown kiwi, and some kaka and kakariki (parakeets), but these may be losing out to the colourful, loud and aggressive introduced parrot, the rosella.

Kokako are also present at Waipoua, though you would be lucky indeed to hear one.

NIC BISHOP

Native wood pigeon, kereru

MIMIWHANGATA COASTAL PARK

Features
Beaches and islands, New Zealand dotterels, brown teal, tidal platforms, coastal lookouts, pohutukawa.

How to get there
Mimiwhangata Bay is about 50km north of Whangarei. Turn off Highway 1 at Whakapara and follow the sealed road to Helena Bay, then take a narrow, winding, unsealed road over a bush saddle to the coastal park. There is a carpark, information board, toilet and ranger station.

Walking time
3-4 hours return to walk the peninsula circuit *or* the coastal lookout and Waikahoa Bay. You could easily spend a whole day pottering among the coves. Strictly no dogs allowed.

There is no shortage of lovely beaches in Northland, but even by this province's high standards Mimiwhangata Bay has a ridiculously perfect beach landscape. It is remote and relaxed, with long sandy bays ending in headlands covered with pohutukawa. Offshore islands hang around the coast and the coastal traders that chug languidly by are the only reminder that there is another world, somewhere.

It's a lazy landscape and there's no particular walking plot. The signposting is adequate but discreet, and a copy of the pamphlet that you can pick up at the carpark is helpful in navigating around this peninsula. In general you can walk anywhere, but use the stiles and don't disturb the stock.

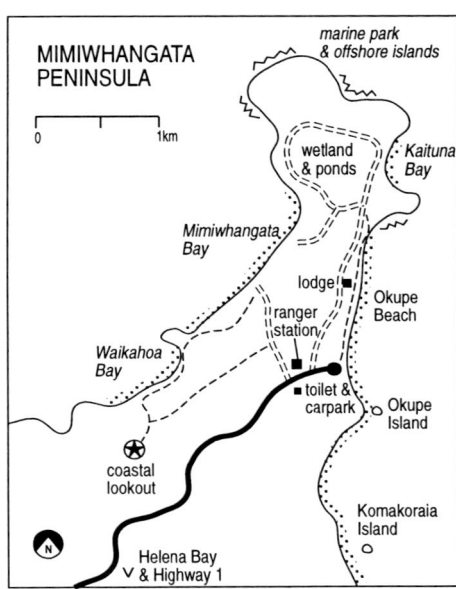

Mimiwhangata is a number of things to a number of people. It is run by the Department of Conservation as an important wildlife reserve, particularly for the brown kiwi, the rare New Zealand dotterel and brown teal. You should spot the dotterel, which usually kicks up a fuss if you get too close, and puts on an elaborate broken-wing display for all intruders. This little wading bird is unique to New Zealand, and low in numbers, so please withdraw.

The brown teal enjoy the inland wetland and artificial ponds, along with the visible and noisy paradise ducks and the poking-about pukeko. The spotless crake and bittern are much more shy.

26

Brown teal

There are several pockets of coastal forest made up of trees such as kohekohe, kanuka and totara, and also some karaka and puriri.

A marine park surrounds the coast and islands. No commercial fishing is allowed and there are strict rules for the recreational fisher. The area is popular with divers.

Mimiwhangata is also a farm park. Cattle and sheep graze down to the land's edge, but do not get to stray onto the beaches, which are fortunately the prerogative of the human visitor. One can sense that the sheep are smugly aware that they are on to a good thing and tend to shift very lazily out of the walker's way.

For a closer look at the peninsula it is an easy stroll along Okupe Beach past the lodge to the headland, where you can pick up a vehicle track over to Kaituna Bay. Eastern rosellas are often making a bizarre and colourful noise in the pohutukawa trees and kaka sometimes come in from the offshore islands. You can take a closer look at the ponds, or else follow the vehicle track as it circles the wetland and you get excellent views along the coast. Welcome swallows and pipits flit about the headlands. Another vehicle track leads down to the wide Mimiwhangata Bay and about halfway along, a gravel road leads over the saddle and back to the ranger station and carpark.

From Mimiwhangata Bay it's a good walk over the next headland to the sheltered Waikahoa Bay, where camping is permitted. Kingfishers are often perched on tree limbs making their distinctive 'kek kek kek' call, and fantails and grey warblers are always about. Paradise ducks raise their chicks here, and seem quite happy dabbling in the sea.

Following the shoreline a signposted bush track which clambers up a kanuka spur to a lookout point. The platform has been removed but the views are still good. A ridge track offers an alternative exit through bush and farmland (and past some massive pohutukawa trees) down to the road saddle and back to the ranger station and carpark.

Somewhere on dusk, back up the dusty road out of Mimiwhangata you catch a last glimpse in the rear-view mirror of an island-sprinkled sea.

BRET McKAY / PROJECT CRIMSON

POHUTUKAWA

The pohutukawa is one of the icons of Northland – indeed, of New Zealand. A thin crimson line between the sea and the bach. Its tenacious, articulate limbs seem to mutter when the coastal breezes blow and underneath the cool canopy the sunlight becomes tinged with a silvery and ghostly sadness. It's easy to imagine why the Maori thought spirits inhabited these trees, like wise old grey heads, endlessly patient, waiting for the tides.

Yet we seem to destroy the things we love and the pohutukawa has been under threat from coastal developers, browsing stock and vandalism. Like their rata cousins, they are also favoured by possums. The Department of Conservation and Carter Holt Harvey established Project Crimson in 1990 to protect the existing pohutukawa and plant more young trees.

Pohutukawa belong to the huge myrtle family, which include eucalypts, feijoa, guava, kanuka and rata. They are salt-tolerant, which explains their pre-eminent coastal situation, but frost-tender as young trees. Pohutukawa have a low seed fertility of 10 per cent, and are very susceptible to fire damage. However, with some human management, pohutukawa will grow freely much further south than their Gisborne boundary and are now common in Wellington and parts of the South Island.

Bees extract a pure white honey from the flowers and some pohutukawa have huge shaggy 'beards' of aerial roots, which only assists the 'old man' image of these gentle shoreline giants.

MANGAWHAI CLIFF

Features
Seacliff and offshore islands, wide sandy beach, rock formations and archway, shag colony, tidal reef platforms.

How to get there
Mangawhai is 130km from Auckland on Highway 1. Turn off at Te Hana or at Kaiwaka (both north of Wellsford), and it's about 20km to the carpark at Mangawhai Heads. Toilets.

Walking time
3-4 hours return. A low, or mid-tide is necessary to do the full circuit. Track closed for lambing August-October.

Beaches are contradictions. They are placid in one sense, with the sand smooth and a passive unchanging horizon, but then there's the restlessness of the surf, and the nagging, subtle invasions of the tide. Human beach visitors seem to share in these contradictions and at Mangawhai you will get the beach snoozers, who defiantly occupy their 20 metres of peace and quiet, and then the surfies, actively and endlessly riding the dream wave.

There is a good energetic circuit walk at Mangawhai that takes you along the top of the coastal cliffs and back down to the tide-line. Those with bare feet will prefer a saunter along the sandy tide-line to the striking rock patterns at the north of the beach.

From the carpark a prominent sign points you in the direction of the beach, and after about 1km there's another sign and some orange poles that climb up a steep grassy spur until you are 150 metres above the beach. The views from the top are superb: the lonely Sail Rock and the Hen and Chicken Islands, particularly Taranga Island with its prominent rock stumps.

On the cliff you are in a mixture of farmland and a coastal forest of nikau palms, puriri, karaka and of course pohutukawa. Tui and bellbirds are vocal, as is the ubiquitous grey warbler with its long trill, a characteristic sound in many North Island forests. Cattle have pugged up the vehicle track in places and the curiosity of these particular beasts is famous, but they are harmless. Like children, they just don't like to miss out on anything, so don't be too disturbed if they lumber up to you.

Mangawhai has had a busy human history. It was a timber port once, and kauri gum was dug from the area from the

MANGAWHAI CLIFF

shag colony

natural archway & tidal platforms

cliff & coastal forest

farm road

spur track

carpark & toilets

Mangawhai Beach

Mangawhai Heads & Highway 1

surf clubhouse

Sentinel Rock

Mangawhai Harbour & estuary

sandspit

Rock shapes, Mangawhai Beach

1880s to the 1920s. The Maori were at Mangawhai long before that of course, and the name is a reference to the stingrays (whai) that frequented the harbour estuary and stream (manga).

The hilltop walking is rolling, easy travel and at one points skirts a natural amphitheatre known as the Giant's Staircase. After 2km or so a sign points you downhill into a gully where the nikau palm seedlings are so thick it's impossible not to step on them. The track winds steeply down a small spur to a cosy rocky cove. There's a pied shag colony to your left and a natural archway on your right.

Although solitary feeders, the shags roost in colonies and at Mangawhai there are about 40-50 birds roosting on three or four pohutukawa. Please don't disturb them by walking underneath. Instead, turn right through the natural archway and there's a marvellous array of rock formations and tide pools to fossick about in. Around two more rocky headlands and you are back on Mangawhai beach, from where it's a long smooth sand walk to the carpark.

It's well worth wandering over to the rocky island, although you can't cross the sea channel. The Waikawau River cuts in closely on this side and there's a good view of the sandspit and the massive sand dunes on the other side. Oystercatchers and the black-backed gull are usually pottering around on the surf edge, and terns (tara) are busy in the surf. As are the endlessly optimistic surfers.

AUCKLAND

GOAT ISLAND

Features
Beach and tidal platforms, marine reserve, coastal cliffs and headlands, sea birds and bush birds.

How to get there
From Auckland it is 90km north to Goat Island. Turn off Highway 1 at Warkworth to Leigh, and drive over the saddle to the carpark. Lookout, toilets and information signs here.

Walking time
1-2 hours beach fossicking, 1-2 hours return on the headland trail.

Goat Island (at Leigh) was created New Zealand's first marine reserve in 1977. Once the waters were chronically over-fished and dominated by a few voracious single species, such as sea-urchins. Now the undersea landscape is lush with kelp forest and thick with kahawai, snapper and blue cod, which have become 'diver positive' and crowd around looking for a handout.

Many different fish species congregate here: red moki, scarlet wrasse, blue maomao, leatherjacket, demoiselles and silver drummer are just a few of the more colourfully named species. Little wonder that even on a dull weekday divers in the full regalia of wetsuit, tanks and mask waddle down to the waterside to enjoy a brief aquatic ballet.

It's a no-take reserve, looking only permitted, and such has been its success that similar marine reserves have sprung up all around the country – at least 10 to date, with more under discussion. Indeed, Goat Island changed the image of marine reserves. They were once so controversial, and are now quite (almost) accepted, but it's curious how the language of the wet world is borrowed from the dry. The sign-boards talk of sponge 'gardens', kelp 'forests' and sea-egg 'clearings'.

For non-aquatic people there is still plenty to see and do. The beach is a lovely strip of sand running north to tidal platforms, and then a boulder shore around to

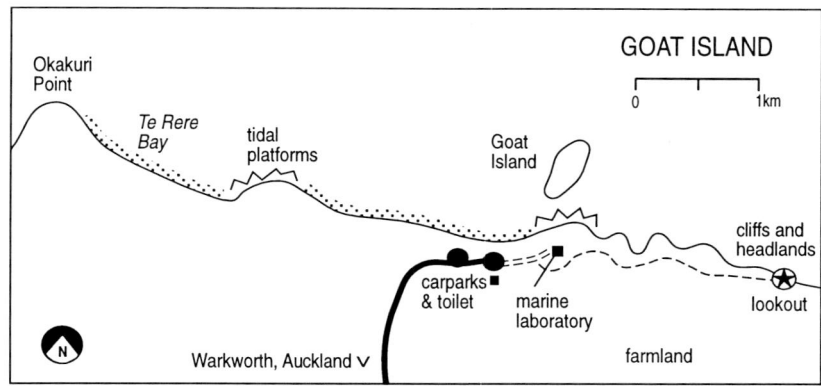

Okari Point. It would take an hour or so to get there, and the reef platforms invariably hold a clutch of pied cormorants perched on the rocks, while terns skim offshore.

You cannot visit the bushy Goat Island itself as no public access is permitted but there are excellent views from the shore, as well as to the lonely Sail Rock, the Hen and Chicken Islands and the hazy bulk of Little Barrier

Seahorse

Island. At the back of the beach the long-limbed pohutukawa provide a peaceful seclusion, apart from the tui, which feed noisily on the flax nectar.

Black-backed gulls are common as are the red-billed gulls, oystercatchers and gannets. Little blue penguins (korara) come ashore in the evenings.

The headland walk goes south from the carpark and follows the road to the marine laboratory briefly before climbing up alongside a fence and following marker poles across cattle-pugged paddocks. The trail is fairly laid-back and continues along a rough grassland path to an obvious lookout seat. Just before here the track has made a discreet turn into cool coastal forest, mainly composed of karaka, tarairi, puriri, nikau palms, with some kahikatea. Kingfishers and welcome swallows are active.

After some bush gullies and three bridges you start getting coastal views again, which get better and better. You are beginning to enjoy yourself when, oddly, the trail just peters out at the top of a steep headland, and private land stops you reaching Cape Rodney. The views of Hauraki Gulf are compensation and with care, it is possible to scramble down the lichen-covered rocks to the tide pools. A pacific place.

KINA

Europeans call them purple sea-eggs, or sea-urchins – prickly brown 'hedgehog' balls found in most tide pools, and lodged stubbornly under a shelf of rock. Maori call them kina and eat the soft insides raw, or cook them in a little fat. You can even buy kina in the shops now, frozen by the dozen. At Goat Island the urchins benefited from the depletion of their natural predators, starfish, crayfish and fish, and in consequence enjoyed a population explosion. Sea-eggs are indiscriminate underwater grazers and got stuck into the kelp forests, which are only now re-establishing themselves. Now it's the turn of the kina to take a hammering as their natural enemies, such as starfish, have returned to the sanctuary of the reserve.

MURIWAI GANNET COLONY

Features

Mainland gannet colony, tidal platforms, wide beach, coastal cliffs and pillow lava.

How to get there

From Auckland follow Highway 16 towards Helensville for 25km, then turn off at Waimauku and drive south-east some 12km to Muriwai. The last stretch of road down to Muriwai is steep and narrow – watch out for pedestrians.

The quickest access to the gannet colony is at Maori Bay carpark, where there are toilets. There is also extensive car-parking by the main beach, plus toilets and an ice-cream shop.

Walking time

Gannet colony circuit (via Maori Bay track) 1 hour, but if you include visits to Maori Bay and Flat Rock add another hour.

The Muriwai gannet colony is one of New Zealand's unique sights. It's rare that you can approach and view nesting sea birds at such close quarters, and it's hard not to compare the scene with a human fishing village. Everyone is related to everyone else, perched on a high wild cliff, squabbling for a good nesting 'posi', gossiping with the neighbours, and keeping their rightful place in the pecking order.

The more famous mainland gannet colony at Cape Kidnappers at Hawke's Bay is a long walk, or a tractor-driven trailer ride. Muriwai is five minutes' stroll.

From Maori Bay carpark an easy track sidles onto Otakamiro Point. Information panels lead you from lookout to lookout as you peer down at the colony. Over your

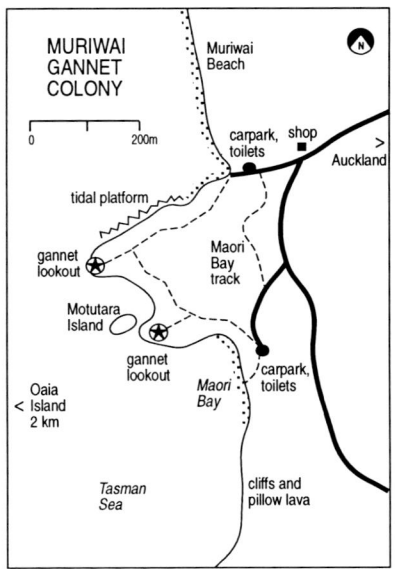

head sweep the arriving and departing birds, taking advantage of the updrafts that make it easy for the large-winged gannets to get to and from the nesting sites. In fact so suitable for gannets is this cliff that the colony is expanding.

It started on the offshore Oaia Island, then shifted to the flat-topped Motutara, 'island of the sea-birds'. Gannet numbers quickly filled this rock-stack and a mainland colony was started. Now outlying colonies of two or three nests are straggling along the cliff edge – you can see these to best advantage from Maori Bay – and it seems quite likely that the viewing platforms may have to be shifted back to give the birds more room.

It's hard to think of another situation where wildlife has flourished so success-

GANNETS – TAKAPU

There are over a thousand nesting pairs of gannets, or takapu, at Muriwai, returning to the same nest each spring. The nest is made of seaweed and grass cemented together with guano. The gannets mate for life and you will sometimes see the elegant courtship ritual. One egg is laid and incubated in turn by each bird, and the blind, naked gannet is born about a month later.

November is a frantic time, with chicks clamouring for food and parents totally pre-occupied in getting it. A gannet's food dive is spectacular: it is often from 30 metres or more at speeds of over a 140 kilometres an hour. The sea is like concrete at that speed but the gannets dive again and again, folding their wings just before impact. They have inflatable air sacs beneath the skin on the breast and neck that cushion them against these constant impacts.

They are after small fish, such as pilchards, mullet and anchovies, which they swallow and regurgitate later for their voracious chicks. The chicks must 'eat like gannets' for by February or March they are ready to leave, usually going to Australia to spend two or three years maturing before returning to the congested tenements of Muriwai.

fully cheek by jowl with humans. The poor white-fronted terns, which originally had Muriwai to themselves, have been pushed to the most perilous ledges.

The track wanders around to a lower viewing platform and then descends to Flat Rock. This place is popular at low tide with the surf fishers, and you can walk out on it, but take care. It's slippery and with a surf breaking is notoriously dangerous. At the beach it's a short walk past the surfing lookout and carpark, then you turn up the Maori Bay track, which climbs through a pleasant bushy gully back to the carpark.

At the far end of Maori Bay carpark there are some impressive volcanic formations of pillow lava. This is formed when hot lava touches seawater, and a glassy skin is melded while the molten rock still flows. As the lava cools it contracts into attractive radiating joints. Muriwai is claimed to have some of the best examples of pillow lava in the world, some of them up to 30 metres across.

Maori Bay itself is well worth a visit. There's a locked access road from the carpark down to the sandy cove, and you can stroll under the dark volcanic cliffs, and back towards the gannet colony. Fur seals occasionally haul ashore from their feeding and resting colony at Oaia Island, where up to 150 seals spend the winter. Frequently you find dead gannets washed up on the beach, a reminder that though the colony is a spectacular free entertainment for us, it's a daily matter of survival for the gannets.

RANGITOTO ISLAND

Features

Volcanic cone, pohutukawa forest, lava fields, mangroves, black-backed gull colonies, rock and sandy bays, coastal views all round.

How to get there

You'll need a boat, and if you do not own one there are daily tour boats that go out for the day. Bookings get heavy on summer weekends.

Walking time

From the wharf to the summit, then McKenzie's Bay and round the coast back to the wharf takes 4 hours. There's no water, so take plenty.

When people think of Auckland two physical icons invariably come to mind: the harbour bridge and Rangitoto. The island would be unremarkable anywhere else, but it sits in the middle of the boaters' freeway of Waitemata Harbour and can be seen from many angles around the city (conferring instant 'desirability' on any real estate so favoured). The shallow cone is silhouetted by the sunrise every morning, and these striking red and yellow dawns are an unwitting if constant reminder of Rangitoto's volcanic origins.

Some 750-800 years ago, within Maori memory, was when Rangitoto last erupted. The first eruption created a proper cone, but successive eruptions smoothed it over and gave the island its broad, flat outline. The full name is Te Rangi i totongia a Tamatekapua: the day the blood of Tamatekapua was shed, a reference to an inter-tribal battle between the Tainui and Arawa.

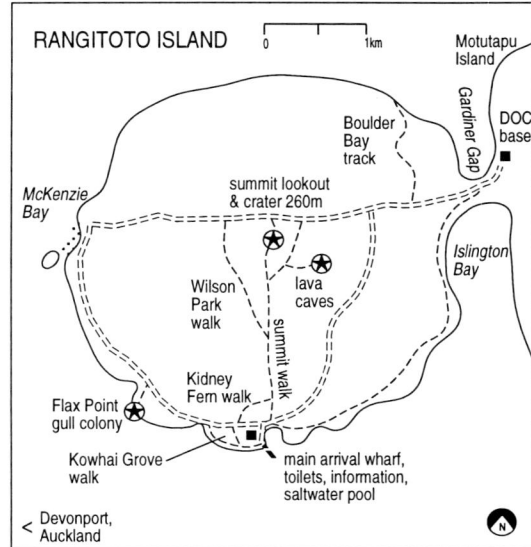

Ferry timetables dominate any walking schedule. Because boatloads of people arrive in regular pulse at the weekend, one gets the impression that the island is thick with visitors. On a normal working day, however, you can seem to have the island's trails to yourself.

The circuit described here is probably the most popular, but there are quite a few other options. To do a full circumnavigation of the island and get back to the ferry in time you would have to be fit, or get up very early. Those wanting to spend more time should consider camping at Home Bay on Motutapu Island, which gives you the weekend to enjoy both islands. See the Department of Conservation for camping permits and prices.

From the wharf go to the head of the small bay and take the Summit Walk. The strange lava fields catch your attention, and if it's a sunny day you'll start to feel the heat as it bounces off the arid black scoria rock. It's an oven, and how any plant life survives without visible soil or moisture is remarkable, and Rangitoto has many unusual plant adaptations. The pohutukawa forest here is the largest of its kind in New Zealand, and takes root in humus-filled crevices in the rock. Once established, the tree provides crucial shade for such plants as mingimingi and koromiko, and these vegetation 'islands' gradually join up to form a conglomerate forest.

There's a track junction going to the Wilson Park Walk but the main walk aims straight ahead. At the second junction it's well worth going down to the lava 'caves', where the outer surface of a lava flow has cooled, leaving a solid skin while the inner fluid drains away. Quite odd.

It's only a few minutes to follow the lava cave track along to the central road and turn back along and up to the summit trig. This will be crowded with people and used to be popular with the wallabies

Pohutukawa and volcanic soil

37

(small kangaroos) that infested the island. Both wallabies and possums have been eliminated on Rangitoto.

Along the central road it's a hot stroll down to McKenzie Bay and you are ready for a swim in the sandy cove. The road rambles along the coast and after half an hour or so there's a turnoff and a short track to a lookout over the black-backed gull colonies at Flax Point. The black-backed gull is the largest of the three gull species in New Zealand (the others being red-billed and black-billed) and this colony is New Zealand's largest seagull rookery, with the chicks breaking out in December and January.

Just on from Flax Point the road crosses an inlet where mangroves have tenaciously attached themselves to the lava rock, an unlikely and successful achievement.

It's not far to the wharf now, and if you have enough time before the ferry leaves it's well worthwhile pottering along the shady Kidney Fern Walk. Rangitoto has 40 species of fern, but the kidney fern is easy to identify because of its likeness to the kidneys you get in butchers' shops. If it's a stinking hot day they will be looking rather sad. And so will you. Ice-creams at the shop!

GULLS

There are three sorts of gull in New Zealand, and they are not exclusively coastal birds. The black-backed gull, or Dominican, is the largest and breeds in small colonies just about anywhere, even on the top slopes of Mount Tarawera. Nests with eggs have been found at 1200 metres, on snow! It is a scavenger and predator, often solitary, eating crustaceans, young chicks and eggs, carrion, offal – anything going.

While black-backed gulls are commonly seen in the mountains, red-billed gulls live mostly by the sea, feeding and living in large squabbling colonies. If there's a gull after your fish bait, chances are it will be a red-bill. The black-billed gull is about the same size as the red-bill, and tends to breed inland on shingle rivers or beside lakes and rivers, but often feeds by the coast, especially in winter.

The book and film 'Jonathan Livingston Seagull' tried to do something for the image of gulls, but it is a losing battle. Gulls fight, squabble, harry other birds to drop their food, scavenge by rubbish dumps, and emit those piercing discordant cries that are as much a part of the seaside as the beating of the waves.

Red-billed gull

38

TAHUNA-TOREA SANDSPIT

Features
Urban walkway, wildlife refuge, sandspit, estuary birds and viewing hide, mangroves and mudflats.

How to get there
The reserve lies in the Auckland suburb of Glendowie, and the main carpark is at the end of the West Tamaki road. There is also access from Vista Crescent and Riddell Road.

Walking time
1-2 hours circuit around the wetland area. You need a low tide to cross the mangrove estuary.

A wildlife refuge in the middle of a city? It sounds like an oxymoron. On an average day at Tahuna-Torea reserve there will be people walking, power-walking, jogging, exercising their dogs (often not on leads), riding horses, fishing, bird-watching and meditating. Youths use the carpark and bird-hide for twilight beer-drinking sessions and there are probably a few marijuana plants secreted somewhere in the scrub. Such intensity of use makes you wonder how the birdlife copes – but somehow it does.

Black shags, grey ducks and pukeko hang about in the wetland ponds, white-faced herons peck about the mudflats, and there are oystercatchers on the sandspit. Tui, welcome swallows and kingfishers inhabit the coastal scrub, and on the brackish lagoon there is a constant vocal chatter from the pied stilts, mallard ducks and paradise ducks.

Flocks of godwits gather in the tidal inlet during the summer months leading up to March, when they nervously prepare for their great migration. Caspian terns, oystercatchers and knots also roost here.

The Tahuna-Torea reserve (or Glendowie sandspit) is tiny – barely 1km long and 500 metres wide, and like a lot of small city reserves seems to have too many tracks for the space allowed. Also jammed in here is a bird-hide by the ponds and a lookout. Tahuna means sandbank; torea is the oystercatcher.

From the carpark at West Tamaki road it is an easy stroll past the ponds, and if you have a low tide it's well worth crossing the tidal outlet direct to the sandspit. At low tide the spit stretches in an elongated curve into the Tamaki estuary, and black-backed gulls and wading birds roost at the far end.

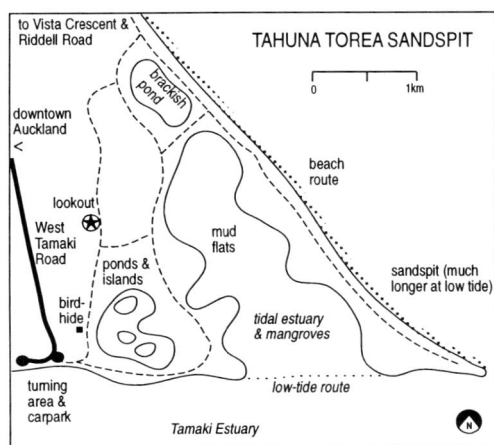

to Vista Crescent & Riddell Road

TAHUNA TOREA SANDSPIT

0   1km

downtown Auckland

beach route

lookout
West Tamaki Road
ponds & islands

mud flats

sandspit (much longer at low tide)

bird-hide

tidal estuary & mangroves

turning area & carpark

low-tide route

Tamaki Estuary

WHITE-FACED HERONS

A sturdy, ubiquitous, self-introduced 1940s import from Australia, the white-faced heron has exploited every possible watery habitat, from shoreline to sewage pond, from riverbank to mangrove swamp. It feeds mostly on crustaceans, insects and small fish and nests in tall trees with a characteristic heron-like platform of twigs and reeds. Although often a solitary feeder, it roosts and nests in colonies. Elegant in manner, both stalking its prey and in flight, the white-faced heron has an uncommonly unrefined call – a sort of harsh guttural 'grr-awww' sound.

White-faced heron in mangroves

Back along the sandspit a trail goes between the brackish pond and the tidal inlet and this is an excellent place to see and hear birds. The ponds were originally Maori fish traps. There's a choice of track back to the West Tamaki carpark, and a lookout over the estuary. The bird-hide seems almost superfluous, you can hardly miss seeing the birds.

FAIRY FALLS

Features
Waterfall cascade, kauri and native bush, historic coach road.

How to there
From Auckland central it's about 20km through the suburb of Titirangi and along the scenic drive past the splendid Arataki Information Centre to the Fairy Falls carpark and sign. There's another small carpark and entrance off the Mountain Road. If you are new to Auckland you are going to need a good road map.

Walking time
2-3 hours for circuit.

This is an intimate bush circuit walk, with well-signposted tracks and a rich forest of tree ferns, nikau palms, young kauri and rimu. Fairy Falls are pretty, cascading down in many short leaps with small pools interrupting the descent. The water volume is not great, but the design has style.

From the top carpark the track quickly reaches a junction, and the main trail turns down an easy spur with many tree ferns. Rosellas are often making a din in the treetops. Past the Goodfellow track junction, the track turns into a stream gully and crosses Fairy Falls Stream, and then starts to follow a series of steps and platforms beside the Fairy Falls.

Fairy Falls   *Track platforms and kauri tree*

41

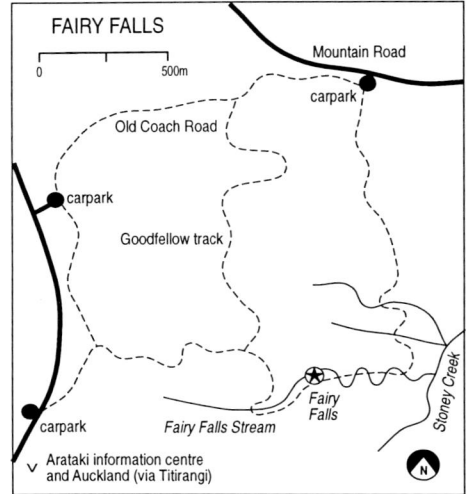

FAIRY FALLS
0 — 500m
Mountain Road
carpark
Old Coach Road
carpark
Goodfellow track
carpark   Fairy Falls Stream
Fairy Falls
Stoney Creek
V Arataki information centre
and Auckland (via Titirangi)
N

There are about seven or eight short waterfall leaps in all, then you cross at the bottom of one leap (there's a wire safety-rail) and scramble steeply down to the base of the last and longest waterfall. A large pool is very tempting for a swim on a hot day.

The track then criss-crosses the Fairy Falls Creek as it goes downstream (you should be able to avoid wet feet), and sidles out of the stream valley and in and out of two more attractive stream gullies. The track is now better graded and slowly starts to climb up towards the Mountain Road carpark.

Here, turn on to the historic coach road, which is wide and easy to follow, but quite steep. You would think the old horse coaches would have had quite a job getting up here. The track crosses two private driveways (keep an eye out for track junctions), and passes the other end of the Goodfellow Track. Now the coach road gets flatter and you can hear the cars on the scenic drive. There's a large off-road carpark and it's another five or 10 minutes along the top track back to the junction to the Fairy Falls carpark.

NEW BIRDS ON THE BLOCK

At what point does an introduced bird became a native? Technically never. An endemic bird breeds only in New Zealand, a native bird is one that breeds naturally in New Zealand and elsewhere, an introduced bird is one that has been brought in, and even though it breeds in New Zealand it would not have found its way naturally to this country without assistance. These technical quibbles may seem slightly pointless when you consider that the introduced birds are here, and are part and parcel of the New Zealand landscape.

Like the Americans in the Second World War, introduced birds have been criticised as being over-sexed, over-loud and over here, and there are quite a few of them about Fairy Falls. Magpies, mynas, starlings, sparrows, chaffinches, song-thrushes, blackbirds, California quail; and it tends to be true that the successful introduced birds are usually aggressive and have a powerful effect on local birds and insects. The eastern rosella is a colourful Australian parrot that has bred from escaped caged birds and is spreading remorselessly south. It's down to the central North Island now and occupies a niche similar to the native parakeets. Colourful certainly, but what is it doing up there?

WHATIPU BEACH

Features
Coastal scenery and beach plain, headlands, islets and islands, inland lagoons, historic tramway and tunnel, tidal platforms.

How to get there
From downtown Auckland drive to Titirangi and follow the twisting coastal road about 25km past Huia to the north head of Manukau Harbour at Whatipu carpark. Toilets and information board.

Walking time
Allow 2-3 hours return for wandering around Whatipu, and 4 hours return if you are going on to Karekare. The headland walk to Karekare beach involves a scramble and you need a low tide.
(Note: this walk description sticks to the beach area. For further details of the network of tracks in the Waitakere Ranges please consult other guidebooks. The Arataki Information Centre on the scenic drive road has a full selection.)

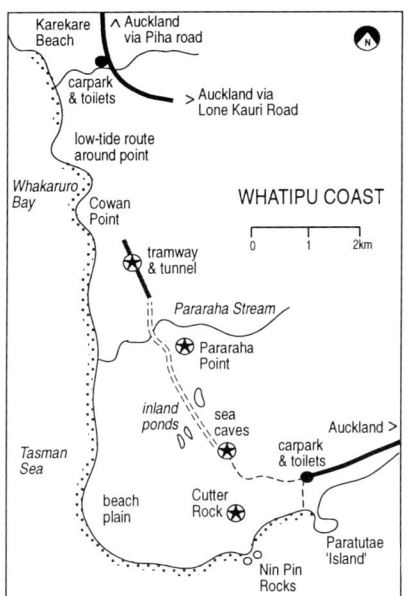

Whatipu is a good antidote to the claustrophobia of town – it's genuinely wild, spacious and sometimes brooding. There is a touch of King Lear about the place: the wind and sea are under a contractual agreement to howl and rage from time to time, usually on weekends.

At the carpark you are immediately presented with choices. On your left a track strolls through pampas grass to Paratutae Island, which is rarely an island. Patient and persistent surf-fishers castoff from the extensive reef platforms that run under the cliff. There's a tiny harbour and an old wharf blasted out of the rock. HMS *Orpheus* was wrecked here in 1963, with the loss of 167 lives – New Zealand's most disastrous shipwreck.

The Ninepin Rocks are popular with rock-pool hunters at low tide and Cutters Rock (this was the shoreline in 1940) sticks out like the proverbial sore thumb, but provides a convenient navigational point for wandering around Whatipu's huge plain. This beach plain is really a sort of a desert, with the attractive jointed rush in thick clumps, almost shoulder-high in places, and various inland ponds. These dry up from time to time but attract waterfowl such as paradise ducks, oystercatchers, the shy bittern, pukeko, New Zealand dotterel and pied stilts.

Jointed rush

A popular walking choice from Whatipu carpark is to follow the track to the sea caves. The Maori used them as shelter and the largest is called Te Ana Ru and the Europeans used it for ballroom dances, though the old dance floor is now five metres under the sand.

A four-wheel drive vehicle road leads north from here past flax-lined dune lakes, which can turn into impromptu wetlands after heavy rain. It's not far to the distinctive prominence of Pararaha Point, where a dark headland traps a wetland and a huge sand dune blocks the valley entrance. Well worth exploring here, with a boardwalk and a track up valley.

If you stay close to the cliffs as you go north you will quickly come across the old kauri loggers' tramline and the historic tunnel. The railway was built in the 1870s to carry kauri timber from Karekare to a wharf at Whatipu.

Camping is allowed here, where several ponds nestle against the bluffs.

Through the tunnel it's easy to follow the tramline past a complexity of small sand dunes covered with marram, lupin and other wild flowers. Cowan Point marks the end of the Whatipu Plain, and leads around the next bay to the unstable conglomerate ('fruit-cake' rock sums it up) bluff at Kaka Point.

You definitely need a low tide here to get across the tidal platforms, and then follow the scrambly track with its somewhat tenuous safety fence. This avoids a small surging sea channel cut in the rock, which you can nip across in low tide if you are quick about it, but the track is probably easier. Remnants of the old tramway can be seen on the tidal platform, then it is round the corner and you are at Karekare.

KAREKARE

Blessed by the fact that houses do not overcrowd the beach, Karekare is a romantic and popular surf beach, dominated by a lonely spur outcrop appropriately called The Watchman. There are tidal platforms at Farley Point and, behind the beach, silent and rather dignified pohutukawa groves. Further back still there's a pretty waterfall and, since there is a connection in many people's minds, toilets by the carpark.

However, compared with Whatipu, where people get quickly lost in the vastness, Karekare is confined and is a serious activity place. Surfers, surf-casters, picnickers, walkers, beach volley-ballers – it's all happening at the weekend. But there are still quiet places for old-fashioned sunbathers to lay down their strip of towel and determinedly do nothing. You will probably drift into a doze, lulled to sleep by the constant surf, and drift into imagining all kinds of sounds. Was that a piano?

WAIKATO & KING COUNTRY

WAIRERE FALLS

Features
153-metre waterfall, bush gorge and stream boulders, escarpment, historic Maori trail.

How to get there
From Te Aroha drive some 25km south beside the bushy escarpment of the Kaimai Range along the straight Te Aroha–Gordon–Okauia Road to a right-angle corner at Goodwin Road. The Wairere Falls carpark is signposted 1km down this unsealed road.

Walking time
2 hours return to waterfall lookout, 3-4 hours return to top of waterfall.

From the Waikato side the Kaimai Ranges form a long formidable escarpment, a natural barrier before the Bay of Plenty. Wairere Falls is a natural break in the mountain defences, and Maori used the route to both barter and bicker with their rival tribes. The Kaimai Ranges were not only a dividing zone for Maori tribes, they are botanically divisive too: the southern limit of kauri and the northern limit of silver beech and kamahi.

The track follows the Wairere Stream in a regenerating forest of kawakawa, rangiora and young rimu. Then it crosses a bridge and edges alongside a farm fence for a short distance before dropping back beside the stream.

The moss and liverworts are thick in this damp bush gorge, and huge round boulders are stacked like marbles in the streambed. There are two more bridges to cross, with some boulder-scrambling in places, and in fact after heavy rain it might be quite tricky to get past one awkward river corner.

After the third bridge the track climbs away from the stream to the foot of a steep staircase with a number of landings to pause on. These steps were designed with giants in mind, and if you have small children in tow it might pay to go in front of them on the way down. The steps can get greasy.

Shortly afterwards there's a side-trail to a lookout platform where you can admire the bush-framed waterfall as it tumbles down in two leaps of 73 and 80 metres.

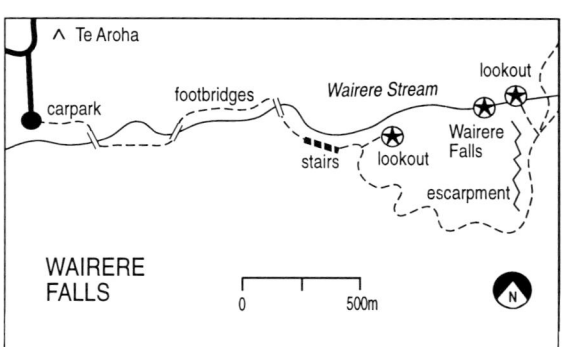

Most people will return to the carpark from here, but the bush track continues to zig-zag steeply up through bush faces to the top of the escarpment. Fantails, wood pigeons, bellbirds, grey warblers and, in season, both the shining and long-tailed cuckoo can be heard.

KAWAKAWA

Kawakawa is one of the most common North Island shrubs, easily identified from its attractive heart-shaped leaves, invariably nibbled with small holes – and therein lies a story. Although it's an inoffensive-looking plant, kawakawa is one of the most potent plants in traditional Maori medicine, and modern chemical analysis supports much of this usage.

The Maori used the medicinal properties of the leaves and bark for treating cuts and stomach aches and a pulp from the leaves helped ease rheumatism. Chewing the leaves also helped to alleviate toothache. Often the leaves were burnt near kumara crops because the acrid smoke discouraged most insect pests, but one insect, the brown looper caterpillar, has built up an immunity to the intense toxins in the leaves and munches away contentedly. So much so that it is hard to find an unbitten kawakawa leaf.

Several Maori trails crossed the Kaimai Ranges, but Wairere was one of the most important. It ran right past the lip of the falls, with early European missionaries being escorted along the same route that modern day-walkers now take. Some of these trails are hundreds of years old and have worn a deep trench in places.

At the top of the cliff the old Maori trail has been utilised to follow along the tall bush escarpment for 15 minutes to a track junction, and a side-trail takes you to the lookout platform at the top of the waterfall. Very good for people with vertigo.

The views of the Waikato are splendid and on a clear day you can see – if not quite forever – the distant glinting peaks of the Tongariro plateau.

MANU BAY & NGARUNUI BEACH

Features
Beaches and coastal scenery, bush reserve, 'tattooed rocks' petroglyphs, tidal platforms.

Reserve (5km west from Raglan on the coast road) or drive to Rangipu at the Raglan Heads. Toilet at Ngarunui Beach beside the surf lookout platform.

How to get there
From Raglan, Manu Bay is 6km west on the coast road. Large rest and picnic areas, carparks and toilets. Access to Ngarunui or Ocean Beach is via the Bryant Memorial

Walking time
From Manu Bay, around the rocks at low tide to Ngarunui Beach, up the bush track and back along the road to Manu Bay 2-3 hours circuit. You need a low tide.

The beach is part of New Zealand's culture and for many city-dwellers one of the few wild places they regularly get to experience. Wild? Admittedly with all the sun umbrellas, picnic hampers, cricket on the radio and all the rest of the beach paraphernalia 'wild' is hardly the right image. There is scarcely a bird in sight, except a black-backed gull eyeing the scrag-end of your sammie.

Yet at Manu Bay and Ngarunui Beach there are over 20 species of shore-bird that come out to feed, usually when the humans have cleared off. White-faced herons on the rocks, pied shags, gulls and terns on the tide-line and bellbirds and tui on the flax headlands. Little blue penguins nest in the scrubby bush right behind your umbrella. They feed during the day and come home only in the late evening.

Manu Bay is popular with surfers, catching the long curls from the Tasman Sea,

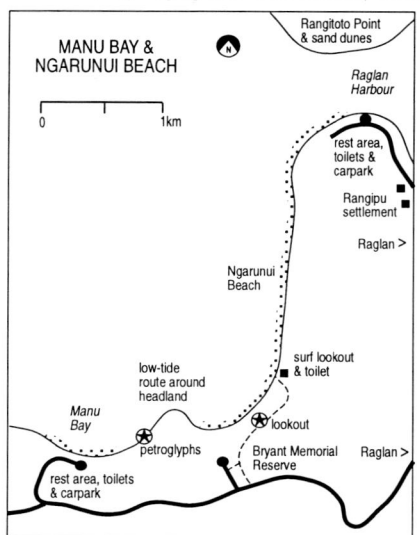

and the foreshore is an excellent place from which to watch their successes and dumpings. At the west end of the bay is an attractive tidal platform and you can boulder-hop along here all the way to Whale Bay.

To get to Ngarunui Beach from Manu Bay there's a fairly long boulder-hop from the carpark, though at low tide you can get onto sand after a while. Just before the headland there are some big boulders scattered on the foreshore; one in particular looks as if it's been split down the middle with an axe. Around here are a number of boulders with petroglyphs scratched on – strange spirals and weaving designs – known locally as the 'tattooed rocks'.

NIC BISHOP

Sand patterns

Much conjecture surrounds the designs and why the Maori drew them. Their age is not certain. The Waikato coast in the Raglan area is particularly rich in coastal petroglyphs and many sites have been identified, though some of the boulders have been removed.

At low tide you can easily scramble around the point and onto the magnificent sweep of sand at Ngarunui or Ocean Beach. The beauty of this beach is that it is relatively inaccessible for vehicles.

Beside the surf lookout tower and toilet is the start of a track that sidles up the hill to a good lookout over the beach. The track goes into the Bryant Memorial Reserve, with one branch going up to a car-turning area on a side-road and the other going direct to the main coast road.

It's a long satisfying walk along Ngarunui Beach to the heads of Raglan Harbour, where there are extensive views of the sand dunes on the North Heads and the harbour itself. There are plenty of spots close to the dunes and cliffs for a piece of solitude, and to linger over the evening sunset.

YELLOW-HEADED SIRFEES

Self-introduced 30 years ago, the sirfee (*Inconstans wavus*) is becoming a familiar creature on New Zealand's coast. It lives in the inter-tidal sand zone and is rarely spotted inland. Sirfees are active in short bursts, with long dormant periods. Usually they hang about in groups, with the males usually active offshore (with a distinctive running, squawking flurry into the water) while the females preen on the shore.

The sirfee migrates north in the winter and is seldom spotted at the same beach more than two or three days in succession. A fickle feeder, it prefers a diet of greasy coastal food, and sometimes it scavenges. Its breeding habits are unknown and rarely witnessed on the beach. A group of sirfees is called a 'surfeit'. They are not shy.

RUAKURI NATURAL TUNNEL
& MANGAPOHUE ARCH

Features

Limestone landscape, natural archways and tunnels, river gorge, glow-worms.

How to get there

For Ruakuri natural tunnel drive 12km north from Te Kuiti to the Waitomo turnoff, then 8km to the Waitomo resort and caves, and a further 1km to Tumutumu Road. Drive 2km along this to a signposted side-road down to a large carpark beside the Waitomo Stream. Shelter and toilets.

For Mangapohu Archway (or natural bridge) continue from Waitomo along the Marokopa road some 20km to the signposted carpark.

Walking time

Ruakuri natural tunnel 2 hours return. Mangapohue Arch 1 hour return.

Waitomo can be translated as 'water' (wai) and 'shaft' (tomo), which sums up the geological situation quite nicely. A bed of limestone runs through the Waitomo Valley and into the Marokopa Valley, and the streams have eaten away at this limestone over a few thousand years, creating any number of fascinating natural features:

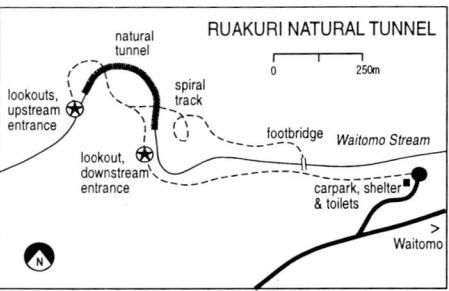

tunnels, sinkholes, archways (a double archway in the case of Mangapohue), caves, 'disappearances' and attractive 'karren' (water-sculpted) shapes in the riverbeds.

Waitomo is famous of course for its glow-worm caves, but that is a strictly commercial enterprise and you have to book a tour to see them. The Aranui Cave can also be seen only on guided tours – book at Waitomo. But the following two short walks are free of charge and full of enchantment, and adults and children will delight in the unexpected whimsies of nature. If you did not believe that nature was neutral, at Waitomo you would think it had a sense of humour.

Ruakuri Natural Tunnel

The Waitomo River runs through a dark damp gorge and almost immediately the track feels closeted. Tawa is dominant and the so-called 'Begonia fern', known as parataniwha, lines the track. This 'fern' is actually a member of the nettle family, fortunately without the sting. At the track junction the arrows direct you firmly one way and you quickly climb up through bush and around a narrow gantry over the Waitomo gorge.

You get a glimpse of the downstream entrance of the natural tunnel before the track cleverly takes you through a limestone 'squeeze' and whisks you over the top

Parataniwha

of the natural 'bridge' and down to several spectacular lookout points.

The landscape can get very confusing, but essentially the tunnel is formed by the Waitomo Stream cutting through the limestone in a small letter 'n' shape.

One viewpoint looks through a hole and gives you a view of the stream in the tunnel, and another (the more spectacular) is on a platform right inside the natural tunnel. Impressive and spooky.

Back in the daylight it's well worth enjoying the dense tawa forest that covers the 'bridge' area, and going down to the last lookout at the upstream end of the tunnel. Be careful around these lookouts, not all are fenced, and those with young children should keep a close watch.

The track returns to the carpark by an even more diabolically clever route. It crosses the natural 'bridge' again, then drops down a steep set of steps and goes under these in a spiral through another limestone 'squeeze' – the kids will love this. The track then wanders along the river edge and crosses a footbridge over the stream (remember, you have already crossed the Waitomo once) and back onto the main track.

Mangapohue Arch

It's hard to know what to call this sort of feature. Is it an archway? A natural bridge? A natural tunnel? Visually it is a combination of all three, with the novelty of a smaller archway inside the main 17m-high tunnel. From the carpark you get little warning of what's ahead. There's a grassy picnic area and then you're into the river gorge, across the footbridge and the tunnel begins.

A good deal of the Mangapohue was once part of an ancient underground river system, most of which has collapsed. The archway is a spectacular remnant, with thick clusters of stalactites on the roof and beams of sunlight that illuminate the walls in rich colours.

The walkway is well constructed, with a lookout platform on top of the inner arch. It's well worth going right through the tunnel to the farmland beyond, where there are picnic areas beside the stream. The sunlight is harsh after the dark tunnel.

Both the Ruakuri walk and the Mangapohue Arch are worth a visit in the evening or at night to see the glow-worms and experience the eerie night sounds of creatures you rather hope not to meet.

PUREORA FOREST

Features
Podocarp forest and lookout tower, kokako, kaka and bush birds.

How to get there
It is about 70km to Pureora Park from Te Kuiti or 55km from Tokoroa, via Highway 30, turning off at well-signposted junctions and driving some 4km to the park head-quarters. Information shelter, carpark and toilets opposite the park HQ. The Totara walk starts just across the road.

For the Forest Tower walk drive north 2km to the Link Road and follow this narrow but well gravelled road (past the Buried Forest turnoff) to a signposted junction after 4km. It's another 500m down a side-road to the carpark.

Walking time
Totara Walk 30 minutes return.
Forest Tower walk 20 minutes return.

Pureora is a rambling, disconnected conservation park on the western side of Lake Taupo. The fringes were extensively logged during the 1960s and 70s and planted in *Pinus radiata*, so to a large extent the remaining native forest is contained on the upper hill country. Old logging roads still provide much of the access to the lowland forest, which is a patchwork of exotic plantations, second-growth clearings and the remaining native timber. These two walks take you into two superb pure stands of lowland forest.

Totara Walk

The Totara Walk starts across the road from the information centre. This short circuit plunges you into the heart of 1000-year-old totara and rimu forest, clustered together in dense supportive stands. You can get a useful information pamphlet from the centre that details the many plants at information stations along the track, and this is a good time to learn some native plant names. The walk is particularly good for the tree ferns, of which four species are represented here: silver fern (ponga), wheki-ponga, katote (soft tree fern), and wheki (rough tree fern).

Forest, like a human con-urbation, is much better org-anised than it looks. As a city has zones for different func-tions, so a forest is organised into layers. Each plant tries to occupy a niche that best suits its requirements. Many mosses, lichens and ferns prefer moist dark places, and tend to be at ground level.

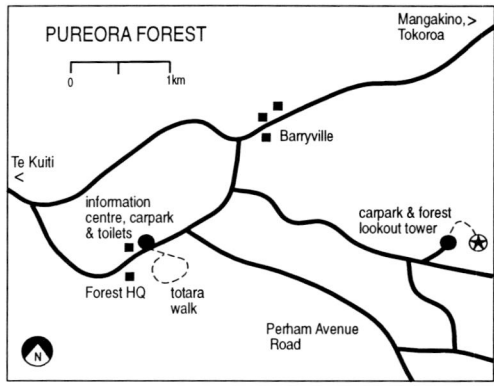

PUREORA FOREST
0   1km
Mangakino, >
Tokoroa
Barryville
Te Kuiti
<
information centre, carpark & toilets
carpark & forest lookout tower
Forest HQ   totara walk
Perham Avenue Road
N

Plants needing more light either grow up to it, for example second-storey shrubs like horopito or pate (seven-finger), or grow on the fringes of clearings where an old tree has fallen. Some plants gain their light by perching on the backs of bigger trees, and these epiphytes are well represented here in the form of perching lilies, ferns and spleenworts.

Many of the big trees are podocarps – totara, rimu, matai, kahikatea, – and grab all the canopy light. In such mature forest, seedlings have trouble establishing and have to wait until one of these forest giants is toppled by old age and creates a 'light well'. It could be a 1000-year wait.

Totara trunk with epyhyte

Forest Tower Walk

It is a short walk through the forest to the man-made lookout tower, and please note the people restrictions on the tower structure. A series of ladders zig-zag up four storeys to the top, where you get excellent views across the top of the second-storey canopy below you. It is disconcerting that the huge rimu tree beside the tower still dwarfs you, and there's still two-thirds of tree to go!

53

'Fiddlehead' on a fern

Suddenly you get a bird's eye feel for the forest. The ground has disappeared and you are in sunny avian strata and from a bird's point of view a lot less threatening than the gloomy ground level: there are branches to be perched on, berries to be eaten.

The tower is a very good place for bird-watching and listening, and it would be surprising if you did not at least hear a kaka. Noisy parakeets are around as well as that brilliantly coloured import, the eastern rosella. There are also kingfishers, grey warblers, bellbirds and shining cuckoos. You would be lucky to hear a kokako, though, which at Pureora, as in many mainland forests, is in severe decline.

Kokako breed from October through to April and their territories are well defended verbally. Two to three chicks may be raised and these fledge in barely a month. The kokako is a wattle-bird, with distinctive blue wattles on the side of its head (pink in juveniles). It is a poor flier and tends to glide downwards, and then clamber and hop up through the branches. For this it needs thick forest, particularly podocarp. If you did hear a kokako from the forest tower you can count yourself blessed: its clear 'flute' call is quite unmistakeable and sounds forever yearning.

THE TREE-DWELLERS

In 1978 a new type of epiphyte was spotted hanging off the great podocarps of Pureora Forest. These particular dwellers were human and the trees were marked for chainsawing that day. This environmental protest against the logging attracted national attention, saved the Pureora giants and significantly increased awareness of the value of native trees.

The Pureora tree-dwelling campaign was an important stage in the growing environmental awareness of New Zealanders. Along with the controversy over the threat to raise Lake Manapouri in the 1960s and the fuss over the logging of West Coast beech in the early 1970s, the Pureora campaign significantly changed public and political attitudes. Logging of native trees has virtually ceased in publicly owned forests and is restricted in private forests.

It is a fact that humans now make or break landscapes as they please – and Pureora survived by the skin of its bark.

KING COUNTRY COAST

Features

Waikawau: coastal cliffs and scenery, black-sand beach, sea birds, historic tunnel. Kiritehere: sandy bay, rock platforms, shellfish fossils.

How to get there

From Highway 3 (about 90km north of New Plymouth) and just inland from Awakino take the left-hand turn-off to Waikawau junction. Drive about 25km on a scenic gravel road, then turn towards the coast on Waikawau Road and travel some 5km to the carpark beside the tunnel.

From here you can continue north to Kiritehere Beach, though access to Kiritehere is easiest from the Waitomo Caves. Drive some 40km on the road to Marokopa, and then over a short saddle and down a side-road to a carpark at the beach. For Waikawau, continue a further 18km on the signposted back-road to Waikawau junction.

Walking time

Waikawau – beach return about 1 hour (it is important to have a low tide). Kiritehere – beach return about 1-2 hours.

One coast, two very different beaches. The entry to Waikawau is gained by a tunnel pierced through a formidable line of dark sea cliffs, and you feel constrained by a huge sea and smooth, inescapable cliffs. It is quite claustrophic. At Kiritehere you can take a deep breath, and almost run down to a long open bay of sand and sun.

The road journey to the coastal King Country should be considered part and parcel of the adventure. There's a sealed road almost all the way to Kiritehere Beach

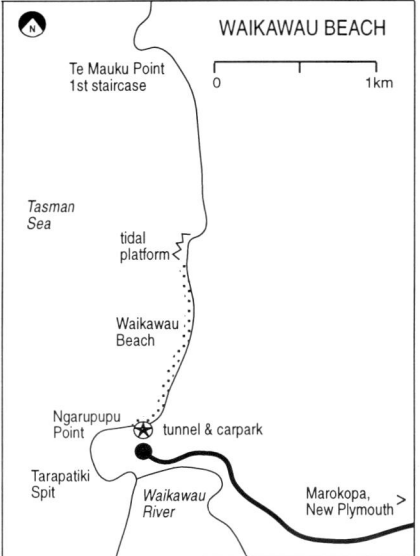

(to just past Marokopa) but Waikawau is metalled and meandering. This is no beaten track; rather a long, engrossing, dusty road through some of the most obscure bushy back country in the North Island, just like the scenery in old settlers' black and white photos. Take your time, take a thermos, take carsick pills for the kids or better still leave them behind – there are no Big Macs on the Marokopa coast.

Waikawau Cliffs

The start is a surprise. It's an historic stock tunnel drilled through the soft cliff, just long enough to make you hesitant before you emerge into a blast of sunlight and foam on the beach. The sands are black and similar to the stuff that they excavate at the giant iron sand works about 40km up the coast at Taharoa.

The scope for walking here is not great, it's just a splendid place to be. A typical west coast surf will be creating banks of soft foam on the water-line, and this ceaseless battering has created some sculpted rock formations along the coast.

With a good low tide you can walk comfortably along the cliff-line to the first rock platform about 1km north of the tunnel. Be warned: the rocks are plastered with a mossy seaweed, as greasy as a rock'n'roller's hairdo. Black-backed gulls will be watching the shore and terns flit in simple grace just inches above a roiling surf.

Waikawau stock tunnel

Kiritehere Beach

Surfers have known about Kiritehere for a long time and there is a perpetual swell heaving onto the 1km band of broad sands. Even midweek there will be some black-suited surfers out there. On the beach you have two choices: stroll north to Te Ruaoteata Point, or go south to the headland where at low tide the tidal rocks contain fossilised clams and mussels. This is a simple uncluttered seascape.

TAUPO & TONGARIRO

Native clematis

HUKA FALLS & CRATERS OF THE MOON

Features
Chasm and waterfall, natural steamfield, fumaroles and boiling mud.

How to get there
From Taupo it is 5km north on Highway 1 to Huka Falls. Carparking and toilets. The turnoff to Craters of the Moon is also off Highway 1, signposted about 4km north of Taupo on the other side of the road and down a short 1km side-road to the carpark, toilets and information shop. Both sites are free entry.

Walking time
Huka Falls 15 minutes return.
Craters of the Moon 1 hour return.

Huka Falls

This is arguably the most visited waterfall in New Zealand, and certainly one of the most impressive. On busy summer days the carpark will be totally jammed with cars, campervans and tour buses. Blobs of ice-cream will be melting on the hot pavements and the passengers on the tour buses will be straight out of the bus and videoing the turbulent waters below them.

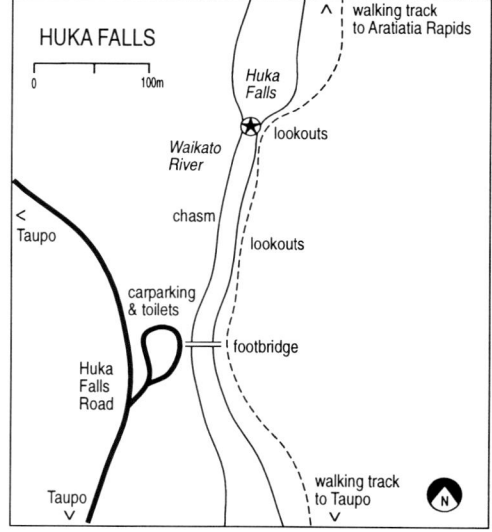

The Waikato River is the longest in New Zealand and pours out of Lake Taupo in a continuous deep blue-green turquoise. The first obstacle it meets is the narrow defile of the Huka Falls, where the normal width of the river has to be concentrated into a chasm about 10 metres across. This causes the normally placid Waikato to accelerate through the gorge in a frothy brilliance of white (huka means foam or froth) and leap over the 11-metre drop of the falls. There are many lookouts from which to appreciate the spectacle.

The Huka Falls is on a longer walkway that stretches from Taupo down to the Aratiatia Rapids. The walk is not especially interesting – mostly pine trees and scrub with views of the Waikato – but for those without transport it is convenient to be able to walk back to Taupo town.

Craters of the Moon

It is a pity that a good number of the thermal areas between Taupo and Rotorua have

Boardwalk, Craters of the Moon

been snapped up by commercial interests and so require an entrance fee. Craters of the Moon is a marvellous exception. It is run by the Department of Conservation, and the hyperbole implied in the title does indicate something of the uniqueness of this hot spot.

It is a steamfield, and large craters give vent to clouds of white steam, sometimes so thick that it is a veritable hot fog of mist. Everywhere the earth surface is alive, and the warnings to keep to the track are serious. Anyone who tries to go off track is immediately alarmed at the deceptive sponginess of the supposed surface. Nothing is to be trusted – keep to the boardwalks.

The track does a circuit through this natural steam field, with lookouts and information panels at appropriate places, showing off the finer points of steam vents, fumaroles, mud craters and the like. There are no active geysers at present (though there were several), but this can change, and indeed such is the liveliness of this spot that changes in the location and activity of steam vents can occur daily.

Umbrella ferns and club mosses, which usually require a frost-free environment, have seized an opportunistic niche provided by the naturally warmer temperatures. Of course it's a risky life and you can see quite a lot of dead roots from plants that got shrivelled when a steam vent opened up beneath them. The common house sparrow darts about, happy anywhere there are tourists and cake crumbs to be had.

Since the forced closure of many of Taupo's private geothermal bores the thermal activity in the Taupo region has noticeably recovered. Partly as a consequence of this, Craters of the Moon has itself become more active in recent years, and indeed may gradually extend its boundaries.

LAKE ROTOPOUNAMU

Features
Bush lake, bush birds, tall podocarps, pumice beaches.

How to get there
From Turangi take Highway 41 3km to the junction with Highway 47A and following

47A over the saddle 6km to the roadside carparks. Traffic can blat along this road so take care when crossing the highway to the track entrance.

Walking time
2 hours return.

Rotopounamu means greenstone lake, (roto 'lake', pounamu 'greenstone'), a poetic reference to the clear and often emerald-coloured water. Different lights create different lake colours, and Rotopounamu can just as easily look a steel blue or a dull grey. It was formed by a landslide some 10,000 years ago, and is about 1km across and 9 metres deep. The bush is dense and tall, with massive examples of rimu, red beech and matai, and the birdlife is prolific. In the morning you can get a real blast of dawn chorus, such as might have been heard before humans arrived in New Zealand.

From the road the track follows an easy grade to a track junction. A step along the right-hand branch brings you to a great viewpoint overlooking Lake Rotoaira. Seats for the already weary.

The track goes down into the dense podocarp forest and onto Five Minute Beach, the first of several white pumice beaches. On a hot day some people try a swim but the water rarely gets above chilly.

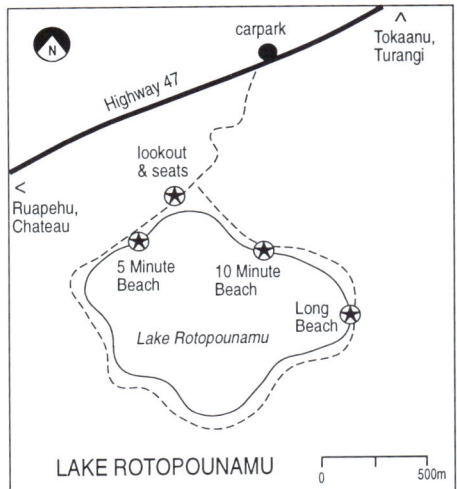

Matai

61

TOKAANU MUD POOLS

This short 15-minute loop walk starts at the Tokaanu hot pools, which are 5km from Turangi. It's a charmer. Steam swirls through the manuka and mud pools go 'plop' unexpectedly beside your feet. There's the smell of a witches' brew about the place, and although the track is well made and fenced, you cannot but help feel a little tentative as you walk – the ground does not feel entirely reliable. The Maori have used these boiling springs for at least 500 years for cooking and restorative bathing in the curative warm waters. Many of the mud pools have individual names and the information panels help interpret the mysterious geology of the underworld.

From here on the track starts its slow circumnavigation of the lake through an array of different forest types. Around Five Minute Beach the bush is mostly kamahi, with lemonwood (tarata) fairly thick, and a side-track investigates a large matai. Known as black pine by the early settlers, these podocarps have distinctive hammer-dent bark.

Quite abruptly the track finds itself in tall red beech forest, with here and there large kahikatea looming up, and rimu 'weeping' in dignified groves.

Ferns abound, with the obvious octopus-looking kiwakiwa on the ground, as well as the taller umbrella fern and the soft filmy fern. Off the trunks of the trees hangs a prominent fern called a hanging spleenwort, but known by the Maori as makawe, which has been translated as 'hair' or 'ringlets'. Spleenwort is an old English name for a type of fern that had a supposed reputation for healing enlarged spleens. The 'wort' is pronounced 'wert'.

At Long Beach you get a break from the bush and this is an excellent spot for a rest and a 'little something' to get you around the rest of the lake. The grey ducks will also be interested in your little something, but dabchicks and shags tend to remain more aloof.

Lakes often have the effect of accentuating sound, which is good news for birdwatchers. Kaka, parakeets, tomtits, bellbirds, long-tailed cuckoos, whiteheads, riflemen, blackbirds, chaffinches, robins, wood pigeons, shining cuckoos, grey

Kiwakiwa

warblers – it is almost a who's who of New Zealand bush birds, and you need a good ear to sort them out. The density of birds here is marvellous, and a sure sign of a healthy forest.

Kidney ferns become more prominent on the shadier side of the lake and occupy wide areas, and kamahi forest starts to dominate again at Ten Minute Beach and back to the track junction. A truly great piece of forest.

KETETAHI SPRINGS

Features
Natural hot pools and fumaroles, tussock landscape and views, beech and totara forest, hut.

How to get there
Ketetahi Springs are on the northern edge of Tongariro National Park. From Turangi take Highway 1 to the Rangipo turnoff, then Highway 47 past Lake Rotoaira to the Ketetahi Springs side-road, about 25km in all. Or from the Chateau take Highways 48 and 47 (some 35km). Carparking, shelter, toilets at road end.

The springs are on Maori land and access is not necessarily permanent or permitted. Check with Department of Conservation at Turangi first.

Walking time
To the bush line 2-3 hours return.
To the hot springs 3-4 hours return.
Beyond the bush edge this is an alpine walk. Take water, as the stream is not drinkable.

People have been tramping to Ketetahi Springs to 'take the waters' for many centuries. The Maori have used the natural hot water for cures of rheumatism and skin diseases, as did some of the early European visitors. These days the springs are just a stop on the well-known Tongariro Crossing, a full-day tramp from the Ketetahi road-end across the volcanic plateaus of Mount Tongariro and down to Mangatepopo on the other side.

This walk takes a more leisurely pace, but it is still a steady climb from the carpark, and allowing for dawdling time over the views, mucking about the hot springs and visiting the hut, you should give yourself a full day – there's plenty to see and do.

The Okahukura Bush is a significant totara forest, with a rich understorey of five-finger, mapou, koromiko and marbleleaf. Crown ferns fill the ground level and um-

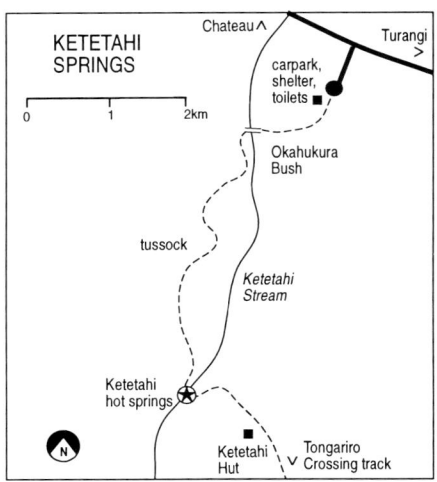

brella ferns and many mosses line the trackside. The track crosses through the forest to a stream, which is un-drinkable, for it's the same stream that has been liberally dosed with chemicals and acids from the hot springs.

There's a side-track to a waterfall cascade and the track meanders around several stream crossings be-fore suddenly getting serious and climbing up a series of steps (and a seat platform) to the bush margin. A seat has been thoughtfully provided from which to enjoy the fine views of Lake Rotoaira and the cone of Mount Pihanga. Over your shoulder you can see the drifting plumes of steam in a gully up the mountainside – Ketetahi Springs.

Turpentine scrub, flax and tussocks now line the track. Pipits become more common, and you might hear the rather shy fern bird, which makes a sort of clicking noise, like two stones chipped together.

It can be hot work on a summer's day getting up the spur to the springs, but on a cool misty day you welcome the opportunity to warm up your toes. Over the years people have dug out or constructed many 'spas'. Usually the best bathing places are close to where the track crosses the hot stream, or even down valley from the track. As you go higher up the stream the water gets hotter and the sulphur smells more pungent.

There is a palette of delicate colours in the streambed: sulphur yellows, acid reds and oranges. In winter the hot valley looks striking across the landscape of snow.

It is about another 10 minutes up to the hut, which has a warden in summer, gas cookers and toilets. A cup of tea on the verandah goes down nicely with the stunning view.

FLOWER OF HADES

Occasionally in this area, usually associated with disturbed or open ground, is found a very odd plant. The flower of hades is unique to New Zealand. It flowers but has no green material, instead living as a parasite on an appropriate shrub, such as *Pseudopanax* (five finger). It feeds on the host root and transforms it in a most peculiar way, creating petals of wood – hence the popular name 'wood rose'. At one time these attractive wooden flowers were so popular that 'daccy' (*Dactylanthus taylorii*) hunters collected and sold them. The Maori name is pua o te reinga, which can be translated as 'fingers or toes of the gods'.

Most of the wood rose is an underground rhizome the size of a fist, and the flower is a thumb-sized set of stalks, looking rather fungus-like, with a sweet daphne-like fragrance. The rich nectar attracts possums, those old villains, which accounts for the significant decline of this remarkable plant. Its distribution nowadays is in the forested areas from East Cape to the central North Island. One further oddity: a study in 1993 showed the prime pollinators of the wood rose were bats. Bats and hades – it seems to fit, somehow.

TARANAKI FALLS

Features

Waterfall and mountain views, red tussock, pumice plains, mountain beech forest.

How to get there

From the Chateau at Whakapapa Village take the short 500-metre side-road to the carpark beside the Skotel.

Walking time

2-3 hours return. Remember this is an alpine walk, so take plenty of warm clothes, a rain-coat and some food. And tell someone where you are going.

This is an excellent introductory walk into the Tongariro National Park, with unblemished mountain views of Ruapehu and Ngauruhoe and a fine waterfall to admire. The colours of the tussock plains around Tongariro are subtle – almost too subtle for the camera. You end up with a photo of a brown-looking plain, which has totally missed the cunning intermixture of reds, yellows,

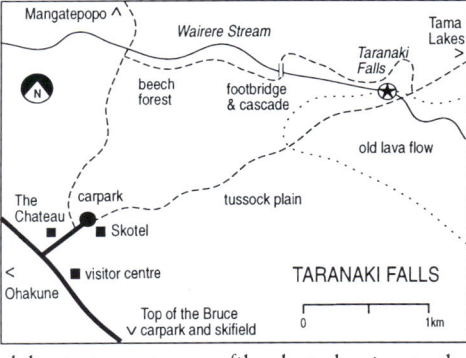

ochres, mustards and purples, too delicate to capture on film, but pleasing to the human eye.

From the carpark the track gives you plenty of time to enjoy the textures as you weave along a well-made trail through fields of tussock and scoria. There are numerous small gullies to cross, with tidy bridges and lively mountain streams, and

Ice and tussock

at one point you climb up on to the edge of an old lava flow, formed about 15,000 years ago. Red tussocks dominate here and look stunning in early morning or late evening light.

By the time you have crossed the lava flow you are at the edge of the Taranaki Falls, which tumble over the thick edge of the andesite lava, without making much impression on it. Pipits are the

Mountain beech flower

most commonly seen alpine bird; their persistent call and constant bobbing from a vantage rock are quite distinct. The early European settlers called them snow thrushes.

There's a footbridge across Wairere Stream and lookout points near the waterfall, though the best photos are from below the falls. The track soon meets a junction and, turning left, you drop sharply down through mountain totara to the base of the waterfall. Plenty of lunch or picnic rocks around here, and on a hot Tongariro summer's day (it does happen) there's no better place.

The track now closely follows the Wairere Stream, first over tussock, then into cool mountain beech forest. Mountain beech has small leaves, with a pointy end, like a peak or mountain – easy to remember.

After the footbridge the stream tumbles in many cascades and there's a short side-track to one of them. The distinctive umbrella fern is found beside the track and the grey warbler and whitehead are common in this forest. Riflemen are also often seen. These tiny, squeaky, chubby birds are immediately endearing.

Turn left at the track junction and you quickly break out of the bush and onto the tussock plain again. The Chateau stands like a proud Swiss matron on the edge of her manicured golf course, and once again the big volcanoes come into view. A few more tussock gullies to cross and you are back at the carpark. The start and finish altitude of your walk is 1140 metres – no wonder the air is bracing.

WAIHOHONU HUT

Features
Volcanic panorama and historic hut, tussock plain, alpine plants, freshwater springs.

How to get there
Along the Desert Road (Highway 1) the turnoff and carpark for Waihohonu is not conspicuous. There is a small sign about 25km north of Waiouru.

Walking time
3-4 hours return to historic hut.

This is an easy but alpine walk, so take warm clothes and some food, and enjoy the spacious tussock plain of the Tongariro plateau. You are already at an altitude of 1000 metres when you get out of the car, and the winds can howl across the Rangipo Desert, and even bring snow in the middle of summer. Definitely a fine-weather trip.

From the carpark you follow an old vehicle track to Te Mako bush, an attractive copse of mountain beech beside the Ohinepango Stream. The water runs clean and fresh, which indeed it should because it is bubbling out of the ground from the Ohinepango Springs some 4km away. You are quickly across the stream and out onto the tussocks again. The views are stupendous.

On the way across the plain it is worth studying the ground-level panorama as well, where multi-coloured scoria mingles with prostrate creeping plants, bunches of hebes and shy alpine flowers. A delicate world within a world.

A patch of bush in the distance resolves itself into a three-way track junction, where the right-hand choice goes past a camping area and across a footbridge up to Waihohonu Hut. Good views from the 20-bunk hut, with gas burners and toilets.

The left-branch track travels about 10 minutes in and out of a large scoria gully and across the Ohinepango Stream to the natural springs. They are nestled in a bush grotto, usually defiantly occupied by a pair of paradise ducks.

The straight-ahead track leads to the old Waihohonu Hut, painted a bright red and well sheltered in a glade of beech forest and manuka scrub. This is listed by the Historic Places Trust as a category 1 hut, one of the few mountain huts to be so designated. Apart from its age (it was built in 1901) it has an unusual construction, for pumice was used as a filler between the double wooden walls. The walls are covered in graffiti, some of it dating back to the 1920s.

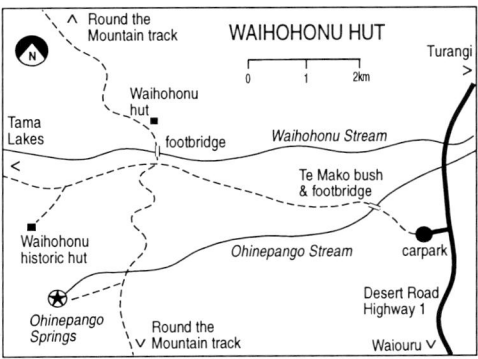

67

Waihohonu Hut

THE CURSE OF THE TOURIST?

Tourism is simply an organised extension of human curiosity, and considering that most of us in our lives will probably play at being tourists several times, there is a surprising underlying note of scorn in the word. Just a passer-by, not staying long, talking funny, with apparently loads of leisure and money. Easy to rip off, easy to dismiss, a 'loopie' on a 'tiki tour'.

On the other hand, tourism is now the world's biggest industry – bigger than agriculture – and many countries depend on it. It brings new ideas, mixes cultures up (for better or worse), spreads economic wealth a little more – from the industrialised countries to poorer countries, from cities to local enterprises. It has made the world smaller and, some say, blander.

In 1901 the Tourist and Health Department built two huts in Tongariro, at Ketetahi and Waihohonu, to provide better facilities for the expected tourism boom. Hardy tourist parties were catching the riverboats up the Wanganui River (viewing the famous 'drop scene') and taking a horse-coach to Tongariro. Waihohonu was known as the Mountain House and was part of the horse-coach route between Waiouru and Tokaanu, albeit on a considerable detour.

The bunkrooms were divided into men's and women's. Getting to Mountain House frequently involved walking most of the way, and this Victorian tourism boom faded during the era of the two great wars and a depression. Turn-of-the-century tourism seems polite, refined and leisurely in comparison to the hustle and bustle of the modern tourism machine.

COROMANDEL

Pohutukawa

CASTLE ROCK

Features
Panorama of Coromandel, volcanic outcrop, bush walk and bush birds, nikau palms.

How to get there
From Coromandel township drive south 4km on Highway 25 to the 309 Road, whch crosses the peninsula to Whitianga. This is a narrow unsealed road but it's only 4km to the Castle Rock turnoff, which is not signposted very well. This is a back-country forestry road, which immediately crosses a concrete ford then climbs steeply. The road is well maintained but would get greasy after rain – first-gear stuff. It's about 2km to the track sign but there's a good turning area and carpark 100 metres further on.

Walking time
2-3 hours return.

Much of Coromandel Peninsula has been logged, burnt and generally worked over until it seems even the second-growth scrub is second growth. The great kauri have mostly gone and have been replaced by pine plantations.

It is ironic that the deforestation of the peninsula has enabled us to appreciate its unusual volcanic geology. The numerous rock plugs that stick out of Coromandel's hills are now not masked by trees, and give a strange and distinctive signature to the Coromandel skyline. Castle Rock is the most dramatic of these volcanic stumps, and with a bit of a scramble most people could get to the top and enjoy one of the best views on the peninsula.

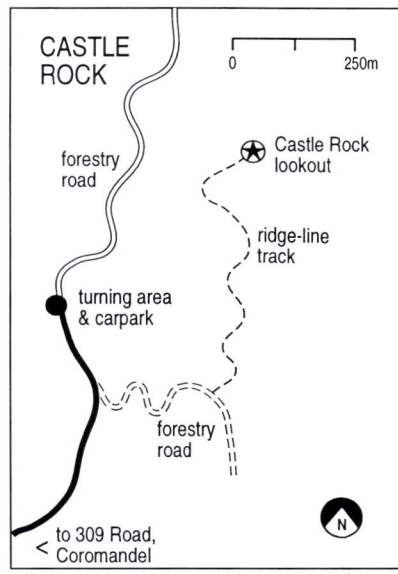

CASTLE ROCK

0   250m

forestry road

Castle Rock lookout

ridge-line track

turning area & carpark

forestry road

to 309 Road, < Coromandel

N

71

RANGIORA

Rangiora is a modest but distinctive shrub. It has larger leaves than any other plant around – big and soft, with a white underside. That has led to the leaf being used as both a sort of bushman's notepaper, and, er ... toilet paper.

The Maori also appreciated the generous size of the leaves and used them for wrapping hangi food, and as a poultice to wounds and sores.

Rangiora flowers quite profusely, and early, in September, which told the Maori it was time to plant the kumara. The white, sweet-smelling flowers attract bees and a kind of honeydew is found on the trunks. A vigorous and adaptable plant, it grows in many North Island forests, native and pine.

From the forestry road a sign points you up a zig-zagging vehicle track through pine trees with a thick understorey of rangiora, silver fern and mamaku. After about 10 minutes or so you meet the ridge-line, and as the vehicle track turns off south, you turn along the unsignposted track north.

You are in mostly regenerating bush, with nikau palms bursting out of the supple-jack and ferns. Birdlife is quite vocal, with grey warblers, shining cuckoos, bellbirds and tomtits. Ironically, it has been noticed that second-growth or regenerating bush often has more birds than mature forest, and it is suspected that this is due to a greater prevalence of fruit-bearing shrubs.

The track is muddy in places and after a while starts to steepen significantly. There are several pseudo-lookouts that serve to remind you that the ridge has become quite narrow. The last part of the track is a bit of a rock scramble, still in the bush and so not especially exposed. Most people should be able to handle it. You really don't get any views till the last metre of climbing, when you burst out on to the summit.

Castle Rock, at 521 metres, is the tallest of a small group of rock outcrops that form a short escarpment. The north edge of Castle Rock is vertical, with an almost 150m drop in places, but experienced people could scramble along a few minutes east to two lower outcrops. On the comfortable flat top there are plenty of places to sit down, have lunch and enjoy the marvellous views.

To the north and right is Whangapoua Harbour, with Great Mercury Island beyond it. On the north and west you can see Coromandel township and the island-sprinkled Coromandel harbour. South there's the Firth of Thames and the main Coromandel Peninsula. East is Whitianga Harbour and Mercury Bay.

When you get back to your car, take some time to visit the small but fine kauri grove just a few kilometres further along the 309 Road. It is clearly signposted. A short, well-maintained track takes you right up to several of these baby giants – not the biggest kauri you will ever see, but impressive nevertheless.

CATHEDRAL COVE

Features

Natural sea arch (see cover photo), sandy coves, coastal cliffs and islands, puriri grove, marine reserve.

How to get there

From Tairua on Highway 25 drive 15km to Whenuakite Junction, then follow the signs a further 10km to the Hahei settlement.

The Cathedral Cove road climbs above Hahei and on to a splendid lookout at the carpark. Toilets and information boards. This walk is often linked with a visit to Hot Water Beach because they are only a short drive apart.

Walking time

2 hours return.

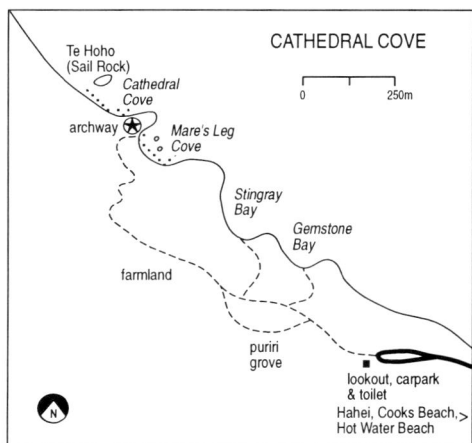

Not many carparks can boast such a view: the brilliant great sweep of Mercury Bay, with its plethora of lovely islands. There are 20 or more, but it is hard to count, and by the time you have counted you've forgotten as your eyes roam to other views. On far land there are gashes of yellow marking more distant beaches, and grey volcanic teeth stick out of steep green hillsides. Almost everywhere you look in Coromandel there's more sea, more islands, more beaches.

If you'd stood on this spot in 1769 you would have seen a European sailing vessel, small by our standards, working its way slowly into the wide-mouthed bay. Cautiously, because its captain was by nature cautious. Captain Cook observed the transit of Mercury here, but one wonders whether he ever dabbled his toes in the warm water. Young Joseph Banks was not so reticent and 'went ashore and botanizd with our usual good success which could not be doubted in a countrey so totaly new', and saw a 'truly romantick' archway.

The Maori have lived along this fertile coast for centuries and there is a fortified pa site right above the archway itself, though it wasn't occupied when Cook visited. There are still the remains of food-storage pits and defensive walls. The coastline around here has always provided abundant food sources and, in recognition of this, Cathedral Cove and Hahei have become the Coromandel's first marine reserve, a no-take reserve.

From the carpark the well-used track wanders in and out of scrubby gullies with pine trees on the hills. There's a sub-track through a puriri grove that's worth taking.

73

These immense trees provide a deep cool against a hot Coromandel day. The settlers found the wood extraordinarily hard.

Further along the main trail there's a short side-track down to Gemstone Bay, mostly a boulder beach known for the semi-precious stones that are sometimes found here. A bit further is another side-track to Stingray Bay. Both bays are quite good for snorkelling, and the water is so clear you could almost drink it.

The main track winds through pines and scrub and then over farmland, where you start to get good views again. The track zig-zags down and dives under the coastal pohutukawa down a flight of steps to Mare's Leg Cove. The odd name for this delightful bay comes from an unusual offshore rock formation shaped like a horse's hind leg, which has since collapsed.

Sensuous rock-sculpted islets sit offshore and initially you feel as if you are trapped between steep rock headlands, before you realise the archway is on your left. This is 20 metres high and 10 metres wide and leads through to Cathedral Cove itself, which is spacious and dominated by Te Hoho, or Sail Rock.

You can walk further around the coast a short way, but it is boulder-hopping and requires some energy. Lie on the beach and save your strength – you are going to need it for the hot, dry slog back up the hill.

THE GHOSTS IN THE PURIRI

At Cathedral Cove the puriri trees provide an ancient shade, where the limbs twist heavily and the leaves rustle at the wind. Puriri groves were often used as burial places by the Maori, and bones were secreted in the hollow trunks. Puriri is famous for its tenacity and doesn't give up life easily. So-called 'dead' stumps can re-sprout if they come in contact with a living root stock, and some trees might equal the age of kauri, for they often withstand the forest fires that kill most native fauna.

The early settlers found the wood of the puriri tree rot- and borer-resistant, and extraordinary hard – 'as tough as a puriri post' was a saying. This 'concrete wood' was used for fenceposts, house piles, railway sleepers, anything that required a long hard life – at a pinch, even the cogs on the driving mechanisms for flour mills.

But the density of the timber does not put off one insect – the puriri moth caterpillar. Whole trees can be riddled with their holes, concealed under a silken cover that mimics the colour of the bark. They emerge as the beautiful emerald green puriri moth, New Zealand's largest winged insect with a wingspan of 100-120mm. Like all moths they have an otherworldly aspect, and must have seemed an uncanny presence under a burial tree.

NIC BISHOP

HOT WATER BEACH

Features

Wide sandy beach, natural hot water spring, sand dunes.

How to get there

From Tairua on Highway 25 drive 15km to Whenuakite Junction, then follow the signs for about 10km to the Hot Water Beach settlement. Toilets and shop at the motor camp. There is another entrance at the Surf Beach carpark 1km before Hot Water Beach.

Walking time

15 minutes return to hot-water spring, 1 hour for digging.

This place is getting famous as the oddity of hot water bubbling up through sand attracts more and more back-packers, campervans and even tour coaches. Sometimes the little springs look rather over-whelmed with people, but the beach itself is spacious, with a wild open line of surf and rustling pohutukawa giving some shade.

It's rare for hot water to bubble up on the coastline, but not unique. There's at least one other regularly used beach hot pool in the North Island, at Te Puia, near Kawhia. But the Coromandel hot springs seem more reliable, and hotter. If you've got bare feet you will soon be jumping around.

The idea is to dig a bowl-like depression big enough to accommodate a number of people, and this should start filling with hot water that seeps in from underneath. Unfortunately this water is usually too hot, so you need also to dig a channel facing the sea to bring in flushes of seawater to boost the water level and cool the temperature of this natural spa pool. Watch the locals – they've been doing it for years.

There is, however, a philosophical problem with hot springs on a beach. If the weather is fine and warm who wants to cook in a hot spring? Yet on a cold grey day the beach is uninviting: drab and windblown. The perfect call is a bright, cold, clear winter's day, a bottle of wine and a damn good shovel.

NIC BISHOP

CABBAGE TREE –
TI KOUKA

Everyone knows cabbage trees. They are an icon of the pastoral landscape, and when every other native thing has been clear-felled off, somehow the gutsy, never-say-die cabbage tree hangs on and thrives.

It is almost a cliché that you can chuck a dead cabbage tree log on the ground and it starts to sprout. The cabbage tree is so resistant to burning that early settlers used the hollowed-out trunks as chimneys in their huts. The Maori used the fibrous leaves for weaving, bird snares, sandals, thatching and rope, and the roots and stems were utilised for food because of their high sugar content. Europeans have looked hard at the cabbage tree commercially, both for paper manufacture and sugar production, but ti kouka plantations do not seem likely at present.

A curious and destructive disease has recently threatened the cabbage tree, particularly in Northland, and efforts are being made to identify the sickness and revegetate dying groves of trees with new stock.

Bellbirds like the fruit and bees collect the nectar. There's a cabbage tree moth, with wings that perfectly mimic the pattern of the leaves, and whose caterpillar makes the familiar notches and holes. And the odd name? Blame that on Captain Cook, who when the crew cooked and tasted the heart pith, they described it as tasting 'something like cabbage'.

OPOUTERE SANDSPIT

Features
Sandspit and beach, mangrove estuary,
Wharekawa wildlife refuge, New Zealand
dotterel.

Walking time
1-2 hours return to the estuary outlet

How to get there
From Whangamata it's about 10km north to
the Opoutere junction, then 3km to the
signposted carpark.

From the carpark the track crosses the
bridge over the mangrove-lined Wahi-
tapu Stream and goes through the pines
to the wild Opoutere Beach. It's a classic
walk, redolent of summer memories as
the children run on ahead to the beach.

It's an easy stroll down to the
Wharekawa estuary and on the
sandspit, where during the summer
there are two fenced wildlife reserves
with a track between them. Please stay
out of the fenced enclosures as these are
breeding places for the endangered
New Zealand dotterel, a thinnish and
noisy white bird, and the variable
oystercatcher, an even noisier bird. You
cannot miss them – they will scream at
you if you get too close.

Behind the wildlife reserves are the
fragile sand dunes, with some rare orange-gold pingao sedge and sand daphne trying to withstand the vigorous marram grass.

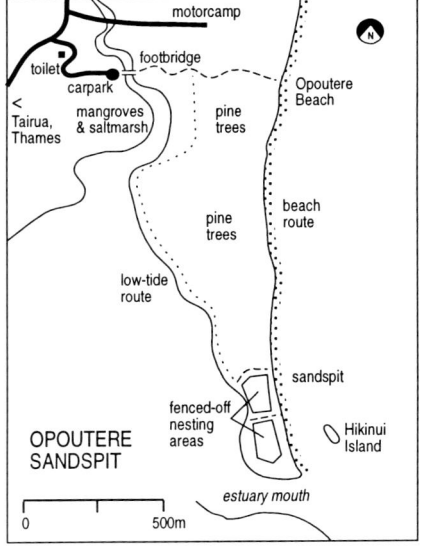

Offshore, Hikinui Island is a haven for the 50-60 nesting pairs of white-fronted
tern, as well as a larger and noisier nesting colony of 100 pairs of red-billed gulls. The
terns are sometimes dubbed sea swallows and are constantly on the move, not
bothering too much with humans. The red-billed gulls, on the other hand, are born
scavengers and take a direct interest in people. It's not curiosity, its hunger! The large
black-backed gull also patrols the beach, looking for scraps from the surf-fishers who
try their luck at the estuary mouth.

At low tide you can follow the shoreline of the estuary back towards the carpark.
The mudflats attract oystercatchers and long-legged pied stilts (poaka). Pied shags

DON HADDEN

NEW ZEALAND DOTTERELS

There are only about 1300 New Zealand dotterels left now, and you will certainly see them in the enclosures at Opoutere if you are here in the breeding season of October to January. If you watch the adults carefully you may see the chicks, which are so well camouflaged that you would never spot them if they didn't move.

New Zealand dotterels prefer a sandspit or flat sandy habitat – just the sort of area that's prone to storm flooding and wind erosion. On top of these natural hazards are the humans who are drawn to these areas – for fishing, for trail-biking, or just sky-larking.

The dotterel lays about three eggs, which take four weeks of brooding to hatch. Then the chicks have to feed themselves, their parents just doing guard duty until the chicks fledge in about 4-5 weeks. It's not an easy life. Any disturbance and the dotterels will feign broken-wing or 'sit down' lure behaviour until the intruder has gone. Too many disturbances and the eggs get cold or, worse, a predator moves in on the chicks. So if the dotterel is trying to lure you away, its time to be lured.

and black shags are often studying the world from a convenient roosting perch, such as a rotting pile.

At some point it's usually easier to turn inland and follow a well-used trail through the pines back to the bridge across the saltmarsh.

At low tide there will invariably be a white-faced heron probing the mudflats here, and in the jointed rush lives a chronically shy bird. If you glimpse (and it will only be a glimpse) a cautious weka-like creature in the salt-marsh you have spotted a banded rail, a bird that has made discretion an art form.

BILLYGOAT TRACK

Features
Mountain views, rock outcrops and bluff, nikau palms, waterfall, historic stone staircases, pack-tracks and ruined trestles.

How to get there
From Thames drive south 2km to the Kauaeranga Valley Road, and follow this attractive valley 13km to the visitor centre and carpark. Note the gate closing times. It is another 9km on a winding unsealed road to the road-end and the start of the Billygoat Circuit. Toilets and information boards.

Walking time
4-5 hours return.

There is a good deal of irony in having a wild walk in an area that has been so devastated by kauri loggers. Between 1870 and 1920 loggers worked the Kauaeranga Valley, leaving scarcely any kauri behind – only the remains of their industry: tramways, inclines, pack-tracks, dams and trestles. The protection offered by the Coromandel Forest Park came rather late in the piece, in 1970, but since then the Kauaeranga has become the recreational focus for the park, with many opportunities for walking and overnight tramping.

The Billygoat circuit has been upgraded to virtually an all-weather track (there are still a couple of fords) and offers a splendid half-day's walking for those people who don't mind a few hills and enjoy mountain prospects. Historically it's a very interesting area.

From the carpark follow the main Pinnacles track as it crosses the Kauaeranga River on a long footbridge and follows the river for 15 minutes at an easy grade through groves of nikau palms. At the junction, take the Pinnacles/Webb Creek track as it climbs steeply up this attractive and narrow stream.

There are several pretty waterfalls in this valley, as well as three swingbridges, and the original hand-cut stone staircases that were built to assist the pack-horses up this steep grade. After rain these steps can be as greasy as a politician's promise.

Bluffs lean over the track as it wriggles up to the open manuka terrace and the second track junction at the Hydro Camp. During the late 1940s workers camped here when establishing the 'hydro line' (powerline) over to the east coast – and the lines are still there. This

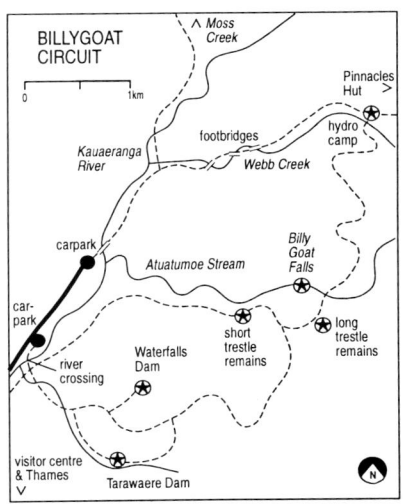

79

Kowhai flowers

area was devastated by a flash flood in 1993.

The Billygoat track starts on the right and follows an old bulldozer line on top of an original historic pack-track up to a saddle. The rock outcrops are a reminder of the volcanic nature of the Coromandel Peninsula, and you get some excellent views over the Kauaeranga Valley. The track winds through thick manuka, young rimu and the occasional juvenile kauri down to the headwaters of the Atuatumoe Stream, where you have to boulder-hop if you want to avoid wet feet.

Shortly on from here is a side-track to the remains of the long trestle – originally 160 metres long and 11 metres above ground at the highest point – blown up by the army for safety reasons and a touch of joie de vivre. The track passes a junction with the Tarawaere Dam track and you get good views of the Billygoat waterfall as the Atuatumoe Stream plunges down a series of cascades.

After some tramway cuttings (and the remains of the short trestle) are passed the gently graded track becomes unreasonably steep and slippery as it follows the historic Billygoat incline. This steep tramway used steam-haulers to lower the kauri logs down to the valley.

Eventually the walking track sees sense, leaves the incline, and becomes pleasantly well-graded again as it winds down to the Kauaeranga River by the old swingbridge. Usually you can boulder-hop directly across the tea-coloured river, and the bridge is only for emergency use. It's about 500 metres back along the road to the carpark.

MANUKA – 'TEA TREE'

One of the most widespread tree-shrubs in New Zealand, and for a long time one of the most disliked. Settlers battled to clear their land, and manuka was regarded as an invasive shrub that undid all their hard work. But times change and the list of beneficial qualities of manuka now far outweigh its perceived disadvantages.

Manuka often acts as a ground cover for other native seedlings, breaking in the exposed ground. It has sweet-smelling flowers that produce nectar and make a fine honey. The medicinal and antiseptic qualities of manuka oil are being steadily exploited and already there is a line of pharmaceutical creams and ointments. And the manuka burns with such a fierceness that people are starting to plant manuka as future firewood lots. And you can always try throwing a handful of fresh leaves into a boiling billy and drinking the 'tea', Captain Cook did – hence the name 'tea tree'.

BAY OF PLENTY & ROTORUA

MOUNT MAUNGANUI

Features

Coastal views and hill lookout, historic pa, tidal rocks and blowhole (Moturiki Island).

How to get there

From Tauranga cross the bridge and drive 2km to Mount Maunganui beach, then to Pilot Bay. Toilets and carpark.

Walking time

Round the coast 1 hour return, to the summit 1 hour return, full circuit 2-3 hours return from Pilot Bay. Moturiki Island 10 minutes return.

From all around the Bay of Plenty you can see the distinctive landscape lump of Mount Maunganui. Despite being only 230 metres high, it rates significantly in the cultural and emotional identity of the district. When locals talk about 'The Mount' they refer also to the sprawling seaside town, that follows an immense sweep of sandy beach and attracts thousands of holidaymakers. In summer the place is packed, the motorcamps are full, and every second car seems to have either a surfboard or a lilo strapped to the roof. The strong, hot Bay of Plenty sun beats down.

This walk description will start from Pilot Bay, go round the coast, then climb up Mount Maunganui via the Oruahine and Waikorere tracks, and descend back down to Pilot Bay via the road: a tidy circuit.

From Pilot Bay the coastal track stays about 50 metres above the coastline, but it's worth going down to look at the historic Pilot Wharf. This tiny stone jetty was the first on Mount Maunganui. Further along the coast track a short side-trail goes down to a pretty sandy beach, where you get good views of the harbour entrance and the Tangaroa statue. This stretch of coast and reef is also an important scientific reserve.

The coast track rounds Stoney Point with good views of the dead-flat Rabbit Island, and you usually pick up a coastal breeze along here. The pohutukawa are dominant, with the heart-shaped leaf of the kawakawa underneath, particularly in the shadier areas. North West Rock is a popular surf-fishing spot, and at low tide you can scramble about the reef platform.

More tidal platforms come into view as you round the corner, with several attractive sandy coves at low tide. The

MOUNT MAUNGANUI

0   500m

coast track

Oruahine track

Northwest Rock

historic stone steps

summit lookout 250 m

lookout

summit road track

Stoney Point

Tangaroa statue

coast track

motor camp

toilets

Pilot Bay

Pilot wharf

Mount Maunganui, Tauranga

Moturiki Island

Tauranga Harbour

track starts to climb slightly and meets a junction just before the motorcamp. This is the Oruahine Track to the summit.

There's a set of historic stone steps, built by the British militia in the 1860s, and another track junction back to the motorcamp. The main track (Oruahine) climbs up onto a grassy plateau with a sprinkling of sheep, and after 10 minutes turns steeply uphill where you meet the Waikorere junction.

Take the left branch as it climbs steadily through regrowth forest, past a side-track to a lookout, and up to the beacon on the summit of the Mount. There are excellent views of course, particularly of the beach, township and Mayor Island.

The Maori know Mount Maunganui as Mauao, and used the hill for many centuries, as a habitation site, then as a lookout and pa refuge. The remains of terraces, storage pits, middens and defence ditches are still visible, though you need a good guide to point them out to you. It's easy walking down the old vehicle track as it winds down through scrub and then farm country, passing a large reservoir before reaching Pilot Bay.

Various imported English birds inhabit the farmland: chaffinches, blackbirds and song thrushes are common, and on the coastal margins will be perched pied shags and the predatory black-backed gull.

Kingfishers can often be spotted around the Mount, particularly at high tide. They eat mostly insects in the summer, but will dine on mud crabs in the cooler months when insects become scarce, and even an occasional slow mouse. When they make a spirited dash after an insect they seem to release brilliant colours from their plumage, and become like the line of poetry by Gerard Manley Hopkins: 'As kingfishers catch fire, dragonflies draw flame.'

OTANEWAINUKU HILL

Features

Dense podocarp forest, pukatea trees, forest lookout, bush birds.

How to get there

You will need a good map but the route is reasonably well signposted. From Tauranga take the Oropi and Mountain roads some 25km, or from Te Puke follow No 2 road some 20km. Or you can follow the Tauranga Direct road about 25km and turn off and travel down the Mangatoi and Mountain Roads some further 12km. Picnic shelter, toilet, small carpark.

Walking time

2-3 hours return.

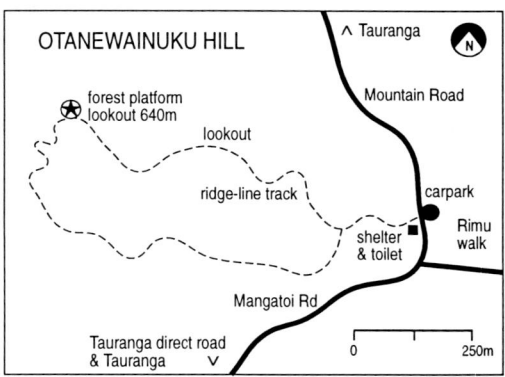

The Otanewainuku Hill does not look like much from a distance, just a bushy volcanic 'island' on the slopes of the ignimbrite Mamaku Plateau. Otanewainuku is a rhyolite volcanic dome, similar to Mount Maunganui. But it has some splendid rimu and tawa forest, the odd kahikatea, some impressive pukatea trees and a dense tangled mat of supplejack vine. The whole forest reeks with lushness, and the birds seem to like it too.

From the rather dingy shelter the track starts inconspicuously and immediately passes two big rimu. At the track junction there's the first of several big pukatea trees, easy to recognise because of their unusual 'flying buttress' root supports. Taking the right-hand option, the track climbs up a ridge with filmy ferns, silver ferns and tall

---

SUPPLEJACK – KAREAO

This sinuous common vine reaches the sun by coiling its black stem around other branches and using them for support. Supplejack leaves are long and glossy, up to 12cm, but we seldom see them, and the fruits are bright red berries. The growing tips of supplejack are edible and have been compared to asparagus. The Maori used kareao for general tying-up duties, such as fences, and to hold thatching in place, and they also used supplejack in the framework of kites. It is not hard to guess the intention of the European name: you have to be supple indeed to negotiate your way through a mass of this vine and most trampers prefer to find a long way round.

Pukatea trunk

tawa trees. The black vine is supplejack and gives the illusion of taking over the forest in a tangle of webs.

There's a signposted side-track to a rather indifferent lookout, but it is much better to carry along the ridge to the forest viewing platform. You are above the tops of the trees so there are wide-ranging views of the coast as far as Whale Island and Mount Maunganui.

From the platform the track drops steeply at first, zig-zagging down through the forest before flattening out.

Wood pigeons abound, as do grey warblers, whitehead, fantails, tomtits, song thrushes, blackbirds and long-tailed cuckoos, with their distinctive 'kraaak' sound, There are also some kiwi here. After a while the track passes more princely pukatea and a king kahikatea before meeting up with the main trail.

Kiokio

KOHI POINT

Features
Ancient Maori pa, seacliffs and sandy coves, shag colony, pohutukawa, tidal platforms.

How to get there
From Whakatane take the road to Ohope Beach, turning off into Otarawairere Road. Veer left at the next junction and drive about 6km to the lookout and carpark.

Walking time
3-4 hours circuit, back via Otarawairere Bay and village and road. Make sure you have a low tide at Otarawairere Bay or you will get wet feet (or worse).

Kohi Point claims to have New Zealand's oldest pa site, Kaputerangi, built between 1070 and 1210. The carpark at 177 metres sits right on the historic pa, which was long associated with Toi, the great navigator. Kohi Point is heavy with history, with at least eight pa sites along the ridge from the carpark to the end of the point and a further four pa along the rugged coastline between Kohi Point and Ohope Beach.

As you walk down the escarpment track of Kohi Point you can still make out some of the typical features of such pa – ditches, terraces and storage pits. Much of this evidence is being overgrown by the shrub forest, notably the rewarewa with its huge and alien-like red flowers. Pohutukawa, manuka, kawakawa, kanuka, rangiora and kamahi are also common, and some puriri in sheltered nooks.

There are fine views looking out over Whakatane and over the turbulent Kohi Point itself with its offshore island and islets crowded with gulls and terns. Shags roost in a colony in pohutukawa trees near the track. The cliff vegetation is stunted, with flax and manuka dominant. The track descends right down the spur to the rock platform at the north end of Otarawairere Bay.

It's an attractive bay, with 'sand' that on closer inspection seems to be composed of zillions of tiny shells. Pohutukawa shade the beach, and there's a picnic area and toilet halfway along. This is where the track to Otarawairere village starts, but before you start climbing, it's well worth fossicking to the south end of the bay.

KOHI POINT

Kohi Point & islands

0   1km

escarpment & pa sites

Whakatane River

Otarawairere Bay

tidal platforms

Whakatane

Kaputerangi Pa site

carpark & lookout

Otarawairere village

carpark & toilets

Ohope Beach

N

Whakatane

REWAREWA

The flowers of the rewarewa are unmistakeable, making it one of the largest and showiest of our native tree-flowers. The tight, profuse bunch of red curls, with bright yellow-red antennae shaped rather like a bottle-brush, is in reality a cluster of individual flowers, with rather an unpleasant smell but yielding an excellent dark honey. The leaves are long and stiff, with saw-like serrations and the Maori used the inner bark to stop bleeding. The rewarewa or New Zealand honeysuckle has rather a 'poplar' or 'columnar' look about it and the flecked wood was put to decorative uses in writing desks and picture frames.

NIC BISHOP

At low tide you can scramble around the rocky islet point, where there are some dramatic geological strata twisted in quite bizarre shapes. You cannot get round to Ohope Beach because a sea-channel cuts right in against the rock, but it's not far along the Ohope track to a good viewpoint from the top of the platform.

The track up to Otarawairere village is actually an old road put in by a film company many years ago, while the Otarawairere village was built as a company village by the Tasman Pulp and Paper Company in the affluent 1960s and boasts some of the best views in the Bay of Plenty. Follow the road back up the lookout and carpark.

TARAWERA FALLS

Features
River cascades and waterfalls, bluffs and escarpment, river 'disappearance'.

How to get there
From Whakatane drive 30km to the timber town of Kawerau, which has a decidedly confusing layout. If you get lost there is a town map outside the information centre. From Whakatane turn onto the River Road (the first left after crossing the Tarawera River) for about 1km, then turn down Waterhouse Street, cross the bridge and continue past the forestry headquarters to a T-junction. Tarawera Falls is well signposted now, but it's still 15km to the carpark.

There's a nice picnic spot just short of the carpark by the Tarawera River.

Tarawera Falls is a public access easement so you do not need a permit to go there, but the gates by the forest headquarters are closed every night. You do need a permit to visit Mount Edgecumbe (free from the forestry headquarters – usually with no problems). Make sure you get clear directions for Mount Edgecumbe from the headquarters.

Walking time
Tarawera Falls 2-3 hours return to the swimming hole, Mount Edgecumbe 2-3 hours return to the summit.

Despite the long drive and the unsealed roads, despite the thundering logging trucks trailing great tubes of wood and sending out dust as if they were rocket engines, despite the fact that you might drive three times around Kawerau wondering if it is some kind of fiendish urban maze, it is worth going to Tarawera Falls. After the stripped and bulldozed landscape it's a relief to arrive into a moist, cool river valley, with the brilliant blue of the Tarawera River sliding silently by.

From the carpark the bush is immediately welcoming, with tui, kingfishers and grey warblers. At the stylish footbridge you can watch the welcome swallows skimming across the waters for insects, and you often see the little black scaup, a permanently 'happy' duck with a smile engraved on its bill like a child's bath toy.

On the other side the track passes through tall tawa and rewarewa forest, with mamaku and silver fern underneath. The trunk of the tree mamaku has distinct oval patches all over it, so it is relatively easy to identify. You can

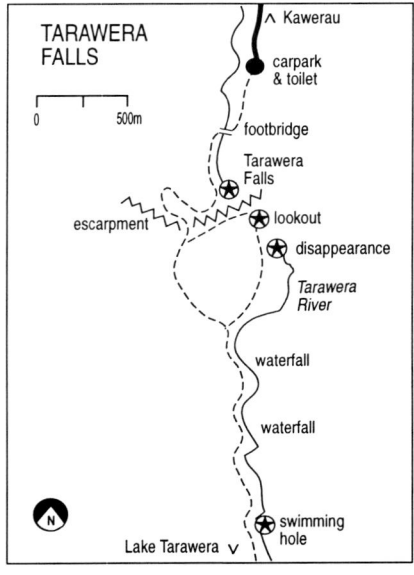

certainly hear the falls now but they are impressive as they churn out from a natural fissure halfway up a rock face. Many people don't go beyond here, but this is really only the start of the magic.

The track starts to climb steeply but is well graded and finds a cunning way through the sheer escarpment walls. Almost immediately on top the track divides and you should take the

Tarawera Falls

left-hander. This is a loop track, which first goes around to a rather stomach-churning lookout directly above the Tarawera Falls, then winds over two bridges and past some pretty streams to 'the disappearance'. Here the Tarawera River, or at least part of it, plunges straight down into a narrow rock cavern.

Resisting the temptation to chuck a rock down the seething hole, continue along the loop track as it closes beside the river and reaches the main drag. The lovely dark bush is littered with massive boulders, which have fallen from the rock bluffs. Tree roots have swarmed over the boulders, and moss and lichens have softened the outlines so that the track wriggles through a rather Tolkienish landscape. In twilight the effect is both magical and sinister.

Quite quickly you reach another roaring waterfall and then, a few minutes further, a second tumbling cascade and waterfall. This is the last of the aqua action. From here the upper valley starts to soften and in another 10 minutes or so there is a massive deep swimming hole, with a platform ready and waiting for you. The Tarawera blue looks as if it were poured from a sapphire gemstone.

MOUNT EDGECUMBE – PUTAUAKI

In many ways Mount Edgecumbe has been spoiled. It boasts no fewer than three sets of steel masts, with telegraphic buildings scattered about, and there is (of course) a four-wheel-drive road to the top. Still, for all that, Putauaki has the romance of an isolated hill, an enclave of bush in a huge organised ocean of pine trees. The views are excellent and there is a curious permanent pond in the second of the double craters, with paradise ducks in the raupo dabbling nonchalantly at 821 metres above sea level.

Features

Volcanic explosion craters, rock colours and scree slide, mountain panorama.

How to get there

Take a map. From Rotorua it's about 20km south on Highway 5 (towards Taupo), then turn off and drive 6km on Highway 38 (towards Murupara). Turn left off the highway and drive 3km down Rere-whakaaitu Road, then turn left into Brett Road for 6km, and finally drive 1km east down Crater Road.

Most cars should not go beyond the bottom carpark, which is about 1km along the road. The vehicle track from here is definitely four-wheel-drive only because it is bumpy and steep in places, frequently gets eroded, and is overgrown with scrub. It's approximately 3km to the higher carpark, which is quite small – it will hold about seven or eight cars.

Because this part of the road, and indeed the whole of Mount Tarawera, is on Maori land, a toll may be collected at this point from walkers and drivers. It is important to note that access is by no means certain and the rules may change from time to time, or the area may close entirely. Make sure you check at the Rotorua information centre first.

Walking time

4-5 hours return from the bottom carpark to the summit. 3-4 hours return to the crater lip.

This is an alpine walk, so take plenty of food and clothing. There is often mist on Mount Tarawera and it is quite easy to get lost or lose the cairned trails. A good topo-graphical map and compass is not a bad idea, especially if the weather looks doubtful. If in doubt, don't stray from the vehicle track.

Mount Tarawera crater

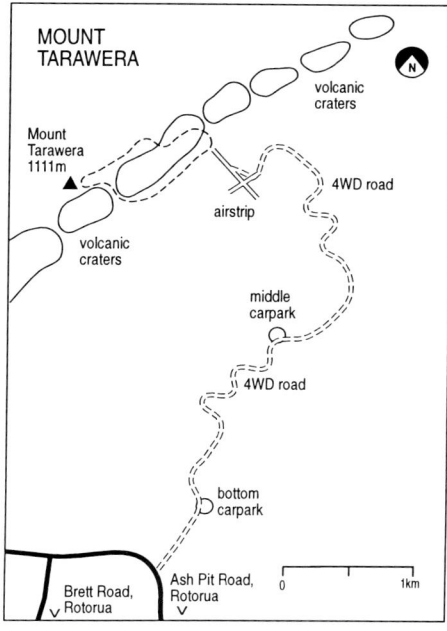

MOUNT TARAWERA

Mount Tarawera 1111m ▲

volcanic craters

volcanic craters

airstrip

4WD road

middle carpark

4WD road

bottom carpark

Brett Road, Rotorua ∨

Ash Pit Road, Rotorua ∨

0   1km

Despite the above warnings and forebodings of doom, many thousands of people visit Mount Tarawera – and you can see why. The line of explosion craters is spectacular, and the colours fairly indescribable... imagine a blood red scree against a bathroom-blue sky and you get the general idea. In many places the scree is a crunchy mixture of reds, blacks, ochres and whites, like some exotic muesli, or a luscious pile of dog biscuits. A landscape good enough to eat.

There is a downside to visiting Mount Tarawera, however. The airstrip on top, the numerous helicopter scenic flights, and the four-wheel-drive vehicles can make the summit area sound like Vietnam on a bad day. This is an area in desperate need of a decent management plan. Peace and quiet are best obtained out of season or early in the morning. In fact on a clear day a crack-of-dawn start (however unappealing) is a sensible idea, as it gets hot on top and it's as dry as a buzzard's crutch.

From the bottom carpark it's good easy walking on the road, past the second/higher/middle carpark and up the scrub slopes to the plateau. Steep in places.

THE BIG BANG

On 10 June 1886 Mount Tarawera erupted. It killed 153 people in villages around the lakesides. It destroyed the Pink and White Terraces, previously made famous by a series of delicately coloured lithographs, and which were beginning to attract worldwide tourist attention. It destroyed some of the mountain itself, but the odd thing is that there's no steaming crater left – not even the wisp of smoke from a hot vent anywhere on the mountain. It blew up and went back to sleep again, and there's no telling when it might blow again.

The whole area from Rotorua to Taupo and Tongariro is a volcanic plateau of tremendous activity, supporting two active volcanoes, three quiet ones, numerous geysers and hot pools, hot streams, soda springs, curative baths and two thermal powered power stations. The area seethes and bubbles underneath, and presumably people who live by volcanoes know the risks, but it seems that every generation forgets. Tarawera is not asleep, it's just building up its strength.

Volcanic rocks

As you get near the airstrip the views become wider, the scrub shrinks away and you emerge on a tussock plain with redpolls and chaffinches flirting in the rocks. Mount Edgecumbe (Putauaki) looks splendid. Across the airstrip you reach the edge of the main crater and sample your first colourful overdose of the red screes.

The best circuit to the summit is around the edge of the western craters, along the trail of footprints, climbing steadily until the trail cuts across the top of a crater in an obvious line. This is a narrow wall between two craters and you get good views on both sides before a sharp scramble through some rocks and you are on the Mount Tarawera summit, 1111 metres high.

As you would expect for a volcano that blew up almost within living memory, there's not a lot growing up here; lichens and small herbs for the most part. Pipits bob up and down on the rocks, and there's a colony of black-backed gulls down to the north. Australian harrier hawks slowly turn above, with their characteristic lazy V-wing silhouette.

Follow down the crater edge (now you are on the other side) for 15 minutes or so, until the trail of footprints disappears through a gap in the crater wall and down into the pit. If you have not tried a scree slide before, you will enjoy this bit. Soft, mushy rock gravels enable you to moon-walk down the slope in a fraction of the time it would take to get up it. The only disadvantage is that you'll have to empty your shoes of gravel at the bottom. Have a close look at these rocks – aerated with bubbles and really quite light from the time they were blasted from the volcanic spout.

The obvious track now climbs slowly out of the crater and back up to the lip, very close to where you started. It's an easy walk down the road, apart from dodging the 4WDs coming up with another load of well-shaken passengers.

UREWERA

Fungi on the forest floor

WHIRINAKI RIVER

Features
River and river canyon, waterfall, tall podocarp forest, bush birds.

How to get there
From Murupara on Highway 38 it's about 16km south to the Minginui turnoff. It's a 7km sealed road to Minginui but you do not have to go into the township itself, turn right over the Whirinaki River bridge to meet the River Road. There's a DOC camping area at this road junction. Follow the River Road upvalley about 7km to the carpark and signboard. Some of the signposting is unclear and it is useful to have the Urewera National Park map.

Walking time
3-4 hours waterfall circuit.

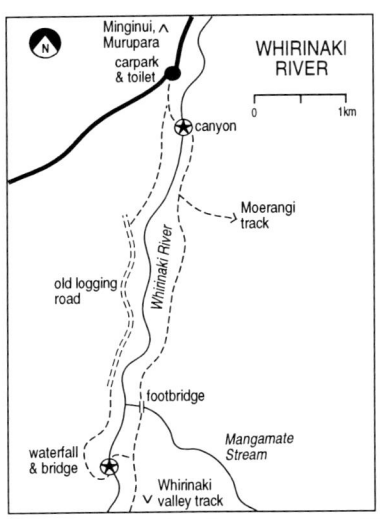

The Whirinaki River is bedded within a damp, temperate and sheltered valley on the western edge of the Urewera National Park. Great native podocarp trees such as rimu, kahikatea, matai and miro grow to extraordinary heights at Whirinaki and in such dense assemblages that you literally cannot see the wood for the trees.

Visitors often liken this forest to a cathedral, as the pillars of wood seem to prop up a grey leaden roof of sky. There is a profound, almost churchy silence. Perhaps the strong winds that normally restrict the height of trees do not reach the interior of Whirinaki, allowing these podocarps to gain that extra margin of access into heaven.

Ironically, it is at the clear-felled carpark that you immediately get a sense of how tall Whirinaki's trees are. From here the Whirinaki track first wanders through the Oriuwaka Ecological Area, a scientific reserve of outstanding podocarp trees, then crosses the Whirinaki River at the Te Whaiti-nui-a-toi canyon. This is deep slot in the rock-bed where the river slicks past the dense greenery.

After the canyon the track settles into an easy grade along the river terrace. You pass the side-track to Moerangi and wander in dark mature forest where the understorey has been thinned out by the dominant canopy – tawa here and there, a sub-strata of tree ferns and a ground layer of ferns, lichens and liverworts. It is spacious and silent, and a relief when a robin lets loose with a volley of territorial calls or a wood pigeon whooshes by. Both the shining and long-tailed cuckoo live in Whirinaki, as well as parakeets, kaka, songthrushes, blackbirds, tui and bellbirds.

RIMU AND THE PODOCARPS

What is a podocarp? They are conifers and instead of flowers produce inconspicuous cones. The podocarp family in New Zealand includes such trees as kahikatea, matai, miro and totara, and podocarps first appeared in the Jurassic period 150 million years ago. A distinctive feature of podocarps is that the seed, which is embedded in a highly palatable fruit, is spread by birds.

Of all the podocarps, perhaps rimu is the best known. Its distinctive 'weeping' leaves give it a signature unlike any other tree in the forest, and it is widespread throughout New Zealand. A mature rimu can reach 60 metres, living for up to 1000 years and retaining its pendulous shape from birth to death. In many places in Whirinaki you cannot easily see the weeping branchlets and have to rely on the stringy, flaky grey bark. Early settlers called rimu 'red pine' and recycled rimu wood is highly sought-after by furniture makers.

There is a footbridge over the Mangamate Stream and not long afterwards a side-track goes down to the Whirinaki waterfall. This is an impressive leap and a viewing platform takes full advantage of it.

A bridge crosses the top of the waterfall to various other vantage points, and this track can be followed back to the carpark. It is not as attractive as the eastern bank, as it passes along an old logging road at one point, but it does make a full circuit.

Whirinaki was at the centre of a famous conservation battle in the 1980s, when all these great podocarps were being eyed up for logging. The dust has settled now, and although the logging of native timber still occurs throughout New Zealand, mostly on private land, Whirinaki is safe. These trees will be left doing what they are very good at – standing tall.

LAKE WAIKAREITI

Features
Luxuriant bush, bush lake and birds.
Ruapani Circuit includes many bush ponds
and wetlands.

How to get there
From Murupara it's 75km to the park visitor
centre and carpark for Lake Waikareiti, or

from Wairoa it's 65km – you pays your
money and takes your choice.

Walking time
2 hours return to Lake Waikareiti. Lake
Ruapani-Lake Waikareiti circuit 5-6 hours.

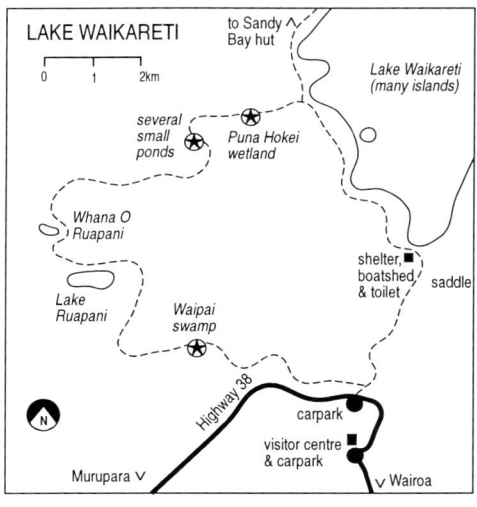

It's a long way to Lake Waikareiti. Highway 38, which passes
through the heart of Urewera
National Park to Lake Waikaremoana, is an unsealed, tortuous
and narrow road. The 100km
gravel stretch is one of the longest in New Zealand and will not
be rushed. Bush lines the road
and in summer the trees turn
white from the dust. Any odd
clearing or settlement has horses
roaming about.

Having survived the road and
finally got to the carpark at Lake
Waikareiti you are ready for
some fresh air, and bush that
doesn't smell of petrol and dust.

The track is well benched and as smooth as a garden path, and indeed the analogy
is not inappropriate for at times it seems that the native bush has arranged itself in a
natural garden. Kiwakiwa (or starfish) fern lines the track, as well as the tall tree ferns
such as the silver fern and wheki. Red beech forest dominates the tree canopy, with
tall rimu specimens poking through.

The bird life is impressive – almost a full forest sound at times: both shining and
long-tailed cuckoos, kaka, parakeets, grey warblers, fantails, tomtits, tui and bellbirds.

The path climbs steadily and reaches a low saddle where there is a toilet and
shortly afterwards a lakeside shelter. A contemplative place for lunch.

Boats can be taken out here (if you have previously arranged a key from the visitor
centre) and it is pleasant sport to potter along the lake fringes and possibly even
reach an island. However, these tin dinghies are not noted for their stability and the
winds can turn Lake Waikareiti into a white-washed miniature sea. Pick your day.

Ruapani Circuit

This grand walk is strictly beyond the ambit of this book, as it is at least 5-6 hours' worth and includes Lake Waikareiti and the many peculiar inland ponds and wetlands.

But if you have the time it's worth it. The forest is consistently beautiful and the ponds have a eerie tranquillity that provides a welcome respite from the all-enclosing bush.

Orchids are often found on the wetland margins and it's surprising to see black-backed gulls and spur-winged plovers at Lake Ruapani.

Some of the smaller ponds dry up and such is the remoteness of the scene that you fully expect to see a moa strolling across the meadow.

NIC BISHOP

Sun orchid

SILVER FERN

An emblem, an icon, a symbol, something New Zealanders will run for, and die for. Along with the matching black shirt the silver fern has a significance that would probably escape a visitor, yet means a lot to many New Zealanders. Why do symbols become symbols? Why choose the humble ponga when we might have chosen the majestic kahikatea, or lovely rimu? Yet along with the kiwi this most mundane of forest ferns proudly represents some sort of unstated emotional patriotism in the consciousness of the country.

The ponga (pronounced 'punga') is one of 10 species of tree fern found throughout most of New Zealand. It is slow-growing, and often looks scrappy in domestic gardens, but can grow up to 10 metres in sheltered forests. The popular name derives from the silvery underside of the leaf, which the Maori travellers broke over to mark tracks. The European settlers built ponga huts and often found the 'dead' stumps would tenaciously re-sprout. Modern gardeners frequently employ ponga logs for edging and landscaping.

PANEKIRI BLUFF

Features
Bush track, red beech forest, bluff lookouts and panorama.

How to get there
See Lake Waikareiti (previous entry). Drive 6km from visitor centre to Onepoto carpark. Extensive rest and picnic areas beside the lake. Toilets, shelter and track information.

Walking time
2-3 hours return from trig lookout (Te Rahui), 4 hours return from Bald Knob lookout.

Lake Waikaremoana is frequently translated as 'sea of rippling waters' – but raging would be more accurate. The winds can howl across this broad lake and send steamrollers of white-caps from one side to the other, and a northerly breeze can concentrate around the Onepoto gap with a ferocity that is disconcerting. Indeed, the first European visitor to the lake in 1840, Reverend Williams, had to wait for several days to make the crossing. Not the first or the last traveller to bide their time waiting for the 'ripples' to subside.

Onepoto has several important geographic and historical features. It's the crucial road saddle, where Highway 38 plunges down to Tuai and Wairoa. The 'saddle' was made naturally by a large landslip that fell off the Ngamoko Range about 2000 years ago and blocked the natural outlet, so creating Lake Waikaremoana. Engineers also took advantage of this event by drilling intake tunnels through the landslip and constructing three power stations at Kaitawa, Tuai and Piripaua. The power scheme was begun in 1923 and was completed in several stages into the 1950s.

The jumble of rocks and overhangs from the original landslip can be enjoyed as part of the Onepoto Caves walk and there is also an historic redoubt at Onepoto, built in 1870 to counter the activities of the Maori leader Te Kooti. Onepoto is also the start of the well-known Lake Waikaremoana track, which circles the lake in a three- or four-day day loop and the Panekiri Bluff walk is the beginning of this track.

From the carpark the track zig-zags past the commodious shelter and onto a flat terrace before entering the bush proper. It's a good track, sometimes muddy or gouged out in places, and it climbs at a steady rate through the red beech forest.

Kamahi, rimu and rangiora are common, as is the distinc-

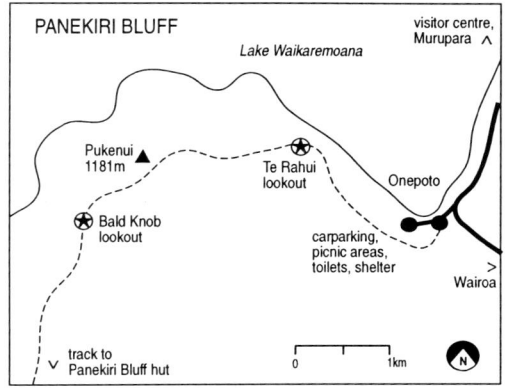

99

CROWN FERN – PIUPIU

Crown fern is ubiquitous. It grows throughout New Zealand, but prefers higher altitudes in the North Island, where it forms a carpet under open beech forest. It has a high concentration of tannins (the bitter chemical found in tea), which seems to make it rather unpalatable to such browsing animals as possums and deer. The reason for the label 'crown' is obvious from its shape and individual plants can grow up to chest height, which is a nuisance to trampers. Maori may have used the bent crown fern leaves as track markers, for when turned over the pale undersides are distinctly visible, even at night.

tive horopito (pepper tree) with its red measle-like blotches on the leaf. Try a bite (not too big) – the strong 'hot' taste is why the early bushmen called it, and used it, as a spice for their inevitable mutton stew. Crown fern dominates the ground level.

Although you get good glimpses of the lake through the trees it's not until the lookout at Te Rahui that you see a first-class panorama, and various rocks provide a good seating 'posi' to enjoy the splendid views. The beacon has been well etched by passers-by. Many people will be satisfied with the views from here and not want to go on.

The main track continues up and down through several minor dips onto a fairly clear area that could be dubbed 'dead tree' lookout. However, for the best views, fitter people need to continue some way further on to the magnificent panorama at Bald Knob, which sits right on top of Panekiri Bluff.

The lake stretches out like a many-faceted diamond, gleaming and glittering in the sunlight.

EAST CAPE & POVERTY BAY

Shag

MAKORORI HEADLAND
& POUAWA ESTUARY

Features

Makorori: coastal views, rock formations, pied shag colony.
Pouawa: estuary, New Zealand dotterels, extensive tidal platforms.

How to get there

From Gisborne take Highway 35 about 10km to the rest area at the north end of Makorori beach. Toilets and shelter.

Pouawa is over the hill another 8km and down a rough side-road to a small carpark by the sand dunes.

Walking time

Makorori headland and return via low-tide route 1-2 hours. Pouawa estuary 1-2 hours exploring. Both walks are best at mid-to low tide.

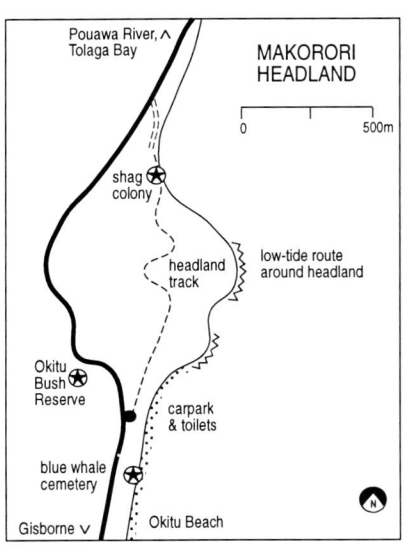

Land shapes its people, and every province in New Zealand has a character of landscape, that subtly shapes the people who live there and the way they live their lives. For the East Cape it is the great bays and beaches – Tolaga, Hicks, Anaura, Whangaparaoa, Waihau.

Once these bays were at the heart of the district's commercial success, since the roads were too slow and difficult (if they existed), and seasick sheep and cattle were exported by lighter through the surf and into offshore boats. Places such as Waipiro Bay were thriving commercial settlements, and one of New Zealand's first cinemas was built here. Relics like the great Tolaga Bay wharf are left as a reminder to the glory days and Waipiro Bay now seems to have more ghosts than people.

Now the slick sealed highway is all and even a modest driver can zip around the East Cape in a few hours — and think they've seen it. But you miss a lot if you stay attached to your car, for every part of the East Cape's coast is charged with drama and sunlight. These two short coastal walks prove the point.

Makorori Headland

From the rest area and carpark at the beach it is an easy walk up onto the Makorori headland. Good views all round, before the track descends back to the beach, and close to a group of pine trees where pied shags roost.

Rock patterns

Assuming you have a low tide it is an easy scramble around the coastal headland, where there is an impressive array of different rock formations: strata in deeply etched layers, rocks shaped like bollards and sea pebbles the size of dinosaur eggs. On the tidal platform the more active of the shags wait patiently for something to happen.

Back at the carpark it is worth strolling to the whale cemetery, where the plaque details the story of how a large pod of blue whales was stranded on this stretch of coast and buried in this large mound. Okitu Bay beach is a fine, long, sandy straight, and much of the way there is a trail through the sand dunes.

Pouawa Estuary
At the Pouawa estuary New Zealand dotterels make a kind of living. In August-September, if their courtship survives the endless disturbance of the trailbikes and four-wheelers, they will make a small nest or 'scrape' on the frail sandy spit. The chicks will be out by October, about two or three in number, and are brilliantly camouflaged, the adults luring away humans with broken-wing behaviour. For six weeks the chicks fossick among the sand, driftwood and coke cans, and fledge some time in November and December, fortunately just before the onslaught of Christmas holidaymakers.

There are extensive reef platforms at Pouawa, and on any good low tide you can see the locals hunting for kina in the exposed rocks. Small sea-channels run through the rocks and seaweed clings like fine hair. It is only a short walk around Pario-konohi Point and another huge beach stretches out, running all the way to Whangara Island. There's no shortage of space and there's nothing to buy or own.

MORERE HOT SPRINGS

Features
Natural hot pools, nikau forest, moss stream, cascades.

How to get there
From Wairoa on Highway 2 it is about 40km to Morere, or 60km south from Gisborne. There is a charge for use of the hot pools, which in practice means that you have to pay to gain access to walk in this reserve. Since most people are keen for a swim anyway this is not a difficulty, but if you object to paying for walking there is a free alternative entrance to the reserve off Tunanui Road and onto the Ridge Track.

Walking time
2-3 hours Mangakawa-hot pools circuit.

Morere is an attractive bush reserve, full of nikau palms and criss-crossed by small gurgling moss streams. The hot pools are in two parts: the lower baths are the biggest, with a swimming pool and attractive glades for picnicking; the upper pools are hotter, smaller and surrounded by deep bush.

From the office and rest areas follow the signs to the Mangakawa Track junction, and start to wander up this gentle spur. The nikau forest is profuse and scatters the sunlight in pools of light. Rimu, totara, tawa, kohekohe are all present, as is the twisting kiekie vine higher up.

The track crosses to the top of another spur and descends this very steeply – you will need your hands here – eventually easing into a moist series of gullies, where mosses and lichens cram every available niche. The track crosses the elegant creek

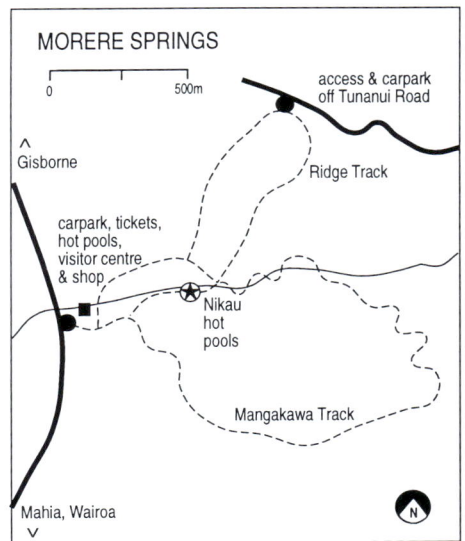

Nikau palms

105

in a small series of bridges
and steps, and will you pass
several small cascades. The
whole streambed seems
alive with greenery as do
several slimy 'hot spots' in
the bush.

Where the creek opens
out slightly you pass a track
junction with Ridge Track
and reach the Nikau Pools.
There are two hot pools
and a cold plunge pool, as
well as changing sheds and

Moss and stream

toilet. The hot pools vary in temperature from 32-40 degrees Celsius, and after the
bush walk are eminently satisfying.

People emerge fairly enervated from the hot pools, but fortunately it is only a short
stroll through the nikau groves down to the main pool and carpark.

THE WORKER AND THE PARASITE

All through the Morere bush you will hear the persistent, undulating, rather off-key
trill of the grey warbler. In the background you may also hear a distinctive rising call
note of the shining cuckoo, with a long tail-off at the end of the song. The two go
together, for the grey warbler is the preferred host for the cuckoo's egg. To be called
a 'cuckold' was a popular Elizabethan insult to a man whose wife might be pregnant
by another man, and the cuckoo's behaviour in England is exactly the same as the
shining cuckoo in New Zealand.

The shining cuckoo is an attractive bird – a ripe metallic green, with an enviable
lifestyle. It winters in New Guinea, the Solomon Islands and Vanuatu, and migrates
(possibly via Australia) to New Zealand in spring. An extraordinary journey of 6000km
for a bird little bigger than a sparrow. After mating the female shining cuckoo locates
a nest (usually a grey warbler's), deposits her own egg and takes off with one of the
grey warbler's egg, probably eating it. The cuckoo chick hatches first – a useful
adaptation – grows fast and within seven days has turfed out the young grey warbler
chicks and monopolised the feeding frenzies of the parents.

By autumn the cuckoo chick is healthy and flying, and ready for the long haul back
to the islands. A continuous summer and a nanny for the kids – not a bad deal for a
shining cuckoo mum.

MAHIA TIDAL PLATFORMS

Features
'Tram track' tidal platforms, sandy coves, sea birds, historic site, old wharf.

How to get there
From Wairoa it is about 40km to Mahia Beach. Starting off on Highway 2 as far as the turnoff at Nuhaka. From the beach it's another 10km across the peninsula to

Mahia village and Auroa Point. From Mahia onwards there are many rest areas and pull-off areas along the shoreline. A low tide is best.

Walking time
1-2 hours for exploring, sunbathing, meditating etc.

As with all peninsulas, at Mahia you can feel a tangible isolation. One translation of Mahia is 'indistinct sounds', an imaginative description of any sea coast where there is a steady and understated murmur of sounds beyond the human ear.

The popular sandy bay at Mahia Beach is backed with hundreds of sometimes lavish summer houses, but over on the other side of the peninsula at Oraka the baches are more homely. Mahia village sits on top of a headland and it is after here that the road closes again to the shoreline and you start to see the array of tidal platforms.

The roads winds around the coast to where there is a picturesque but dodgy fishing wharf, and a few tired boats are anchored in the harbour. Just along from here is the Whangaweri Reserve, a small coastal reserve notable for the hollowed-out stone that

'Tram tracks' in the reef

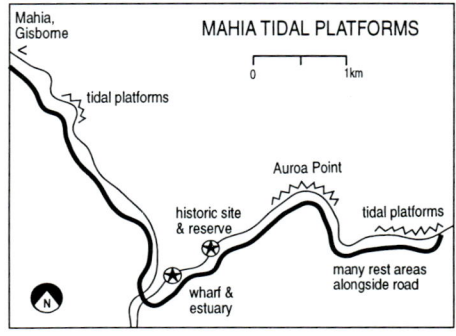

MAHIA TIDAL PLATFORMS

Mahia,
Gisborne

0   1km

tidal platforms

Auroa Point

historic site
& reserve

tidal platforms

many rest areas
alongside road

wharf &
estuary

N

was reputedly used as a baptismal font by the early missionaries when they baptised the local Maori. There are also several small cemeteries enjoying an unparalleled outlook over the sea to the distant Young Nick's Head.

The seal ends here but the road rambles around the open coast at Auroa Point and unexpectedly runs out onto a sandy beach. Pohutukawa and ngaio provide some shade on the foreshore.

All along this coast at low tide the sea reveals a virtual rock-desert of sea reefs and tidal platforms. Long furrows of rock run from the sandy coves out to sea, as if some mad ploughman had decided to have a go at bringing the seabed to pasture. These rock structures have been likened to 'tramlines' and there are hundreds of them, in many unusual permutations of style and colour.

Tide pools become trapped between the crusts of rock and provide temporary micro-habitats for crabs and small fish while the exposed reefs dry out and sizzle in the Mahia sunlight.

While humans stroll about bemused at the geological spectacle, the sea birds get to work. White-faced herons carefully probe the channels of water, and even mynas come down to the water-line looking for small crabs. Black-backed gulls and black shags tend to be solitary feeders, and you might see the sleek gannet do a spectacular dive for fish just offshore.

If you sit in the sun at Mahia you are bound to nod off, as the foreshore tussocks rustle in the sea-breeze and the pied shag spreads its wings to dry.

When you wake up the sea has returned.

NIC BISHOP

Chiton

108

HAWKE'S BAY

Shine Falls

SHINE FALLS & BELL ROCK

Features

Shine Falls: waterfall and sandstone gorge, matai and kamahi forest, escarpment and lookouts.

Bell Rock: podocarp and beech forest, eroded geological features, landscape views.

How to get there

From Napier drive 50km north to Lake Tutira and take the Matahorua road some 5km to the Pohokura road junction. For the shortest walking access to Shine Falls continue on the Matahorua road about another 5km, then take the Heays Access Road another 5km to the carpark and shelter by the sandstone bluffs.

For the western end of the Shine Falls walkway, continue on the Pohokura road as it climbs remorselessly up past limestone outcrops with impressive views of Hawke's Bay. After about 8km you reach a small carpark and signboard for Shine Falls.

For Bell Rock drive another few kilometres to the start of the bush track, and another 1km to Maungaharuru Saddle and the vehicle track access to Bell Rock.

Walking time

Shine Falls from Heays Road 2-3 hours return. Shine Falls entire walking track 4-5 hours one way. Kamahi Loop Track 2-3 hours return.

Bell Rock bush track and return via vehicle track 3-4 hours return. The ridge can be exposed and harsh in bad weather.

The Shine Falls track (or Boundary Stream track) features a great contrast of scenery: sandstone bluffs and rock lookouts, open and airy kanuka groves and dark, dense kamahi bush. There's a charmer of a waterfall, named not from the sheen of water as it slides down the sandstone cliff, but after the Shine family, who were pioneer farmers in this district and donated some of their land to the scenic reserve.

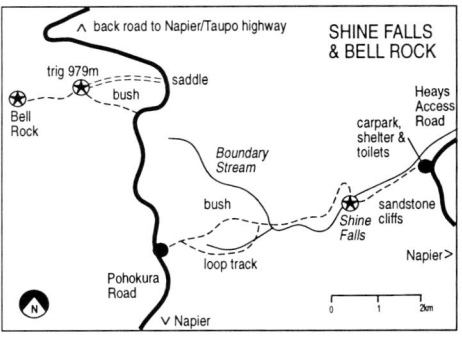

If you are walking the whole length of the Shine Falls track most people start from the Pohokura road, since the track is mostly downhill to Heays Road. At the start of the track there are a couple of enormous matai, said to have been spared by the loggers because they were 'too big'.

At the first track junction the Kamahi Loop Track provides an easier alternative for people who don't want to walk the entire route. The kamahi is dense, dark and almost devoid of understorey plants, so that without the track markers it would be quite easy to get lost here. It is a strange, somewhat sinister forest and it's a relief when the track reaches the cliff margins and the more open manuka.

There are some good views along here before you drop down to the track junction.

The Kamahi Loop Track continues by negotiating up beside a pretty sandstone stream, and at the top picks up an old pack-track (or perhaps a dray road) before it sidles back to the main trail. The main track to Shine Falls descends Goat Hill and passes Castle Rock to Boundary Stream. A small stand of rimu and some large kanuka grow in this damp part of the valley. The track climbs to a terrace through tawa, rewarewa and silver fern, then sidles down to Heays Bluff, with a sharp descent to the base of the 58m Shine Falls.

After crossing the stream the track winds through open bush infested with goats and imported weeds. The plants that have survived the settlers' deforestation and burning, and the introduction of browsing animals tend to be robust, such as kanuka, rangiora, cabbage tree, rewarewa and the heart-shaped kawakawa.

Kiwi and wood pigeons were once reported here in large numbers, but both have declined significantly. Today you are most likely to see the common bush birds such as bellbirds and fantails, along with chaffinches, blackbirds and song thrushes in the forest margins. The last part of the track crosses farmland underneath large sandstone cliffs that turn a gorgeous yellow in the failing evening light.

Bell Rock

This short bush track is unexpectedly lush. Nestled under the ridge and protected from prevailing winds, the track wanders through a dense stand of broadleaf, totara, fuchsia, horopito (pepper tree) and mountain holly. Wood pigeons unnervingly explode through the canopy over your head. If they had the sense to stay still you would never see them. Close to the ridge there is a small impressive stand of red beech, and then you are out on the wind-blasted heights of the Maungaharuru Range.

Poles take you over open farm and tussock slopes past sandstone outcrops (and the occasional hole or 'tomo') down to Bell Rock. Here the topsoil has been exposed by land clearance and burn-offs and been blown away, leaving the soft sandstone underneath to be etched into peculiar shapes. The views from the ridge are superb:

from Napier to Poverty Bay, from Lake Tutira to the hinterland of the Urewera.

Instead of returning by the bush track you can follow the old vehicle road through open grasslands down to the Maungaharuru Saddle (there are some etched wind-eroded rocks here too) and it is about 1km back along the road to the carpark.

Bell Rock

AHURIRI ESTUARY

Features
Estuary and saltmarsh, wading and migrant birds, spoonbills.

How to get there
From Napier city it is 1km to either the Humber Street carpark or alongside Meeanee Quay. Westshore lagoon can be reached from Watchman's Road, and there's a side-road to a carpark, birdhide and picnic area. Note that this area is closed at dusk.

Walking time
1 hour return.

Estuaries are natural food baskets, full of fish, crabs, shellfish and eels, which in turn attract thousands of wading birds – and the predators that feed on them. Maori used Ahuriri estuary as a food-gathering area (mahinga kai) for centuries, and the early Europeans were attracted to the sanctuary of the estuary harbour.

But once the settlers were established and crossed the threshold from simple survival to development then the estuary became a nuisance. It was ditched and drained; wetlands turned into paddocks, saltmarsh into grass. The 1931 Napier earthquake lifted the estuary area so that now the once huge 3800-hectare lagoon, Te Whanganui a Orotu, is now the 380-hectare Ahuriri estuary.

Even this remnant is productive. About 500 million litres of water are transferred into and out of the lagoon at each tide; 55 bird species have been recorded here so far, 30 fish species and 33 types of invertebrates.

THE MIGRANTS

It is a cliché that we live on a shrinking planet. The car that hoons across Pandora bridge in the morning rush-hour could be in Auckland by the end of the day, then the driver could catch a plane to England and be there in less than 24 hours. We might take a journey to the northern hemisphere once in a lifetime – but some of those apparently frail migrant birds dabbling under Pandora bridge do it every single year.

Migrant birds from as far away as Siberia, Alaska and Australia stop over at the Ahuriri estuary, which is only a part of an intricate network of saltwater and freshwater lagoons that are utilised from Parengarenga Harbour at the tip of Northland to the great Southland estuaries of Bluff and Tiwai Point. An avian alternative to petrol stations and rest areas.

Why birds such as the godwit and turnstone travel from the Arctic to winter over in New Zealand is not clear, and how they get here is something of a puzzle too. Perhaps they use the stars or sun, or sense the magnetic fields emanating from the planet. For some the Ahuriri estuary is just a café stop, for others it is a major refuelling stop. Some use the estuary as a winter feeding ground, starting to leave as we leaf through the autumn holiday catalogues on Fiji. The migrants take a month or so to fly 12,000 kilometres to their breeding ground in Siberia, with no in-flight service.

Spur-winged plover

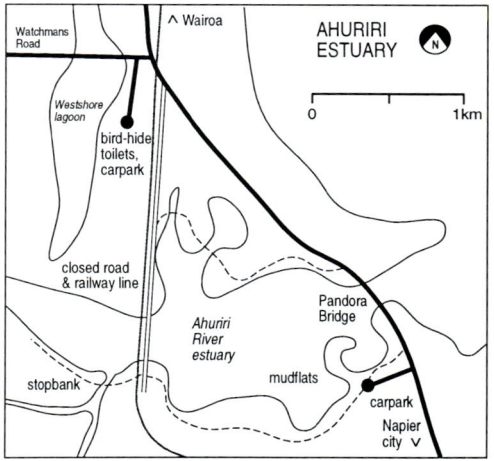

This whole walk circuit takes only an hour and there are several excellent interpretation signboards. From the Humber Street carpark the track crosses a footbridge and skirts a line of factories past plantings of ngaio and eucalypts. After about 15 minutes the track reaches the embankment bridge, which is closed to cars and has created an excellent viewing platform for the estuary and river.

An unmarked side-track crosses a water-control gate and follows a stopbank alongside the upper Ahuriri lagoon, a good place to look out for roosting spoonbills.

The main track continues over the road bridge and winds over boardwalks through saltmarsh ponds and subtle textures of glasswort (ureure) back around to Meeanee Quay and Pandora bridge.

WAIMARAMA BEACH & BARE ISLAND

Features
Coastal scenery and islands, sandy picnic bay, concretions and glamorous geology.

How to get there
From Hastings travel through Havelock North and on a good sealed road some 20km to Waimarama Beach and the carpark at the south end, well signposted.

Walking time
2-3 hours return to Cray Bay 4-5 hours return to Red Island. Because of the boulder-hopping this walk is not suited for the less agile.

It is essential to have a *low tide* as there are precious few escape routes up the steep clay cliffs. If you get to Cray Bay and the tide is beating you, it is possible to climb up onto the cliff edge here and follow the pine trees back to Waimarama.

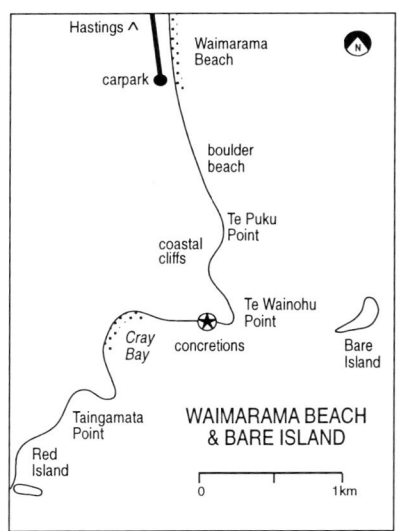

This coastal walk is hard work and the lower the tide the better, as it exposes strips of sand that make the walking a lot easier. The compensations are a fine piece of coast, a lovely sandy beach at Cray Bay, and a giant collection of stone marbles at Te Wainohu Point called concretions. There's also a bewildering array of patterned rocks all along the coastline and you don't have to be a geologist to enjoy them. (Please do not take rock specimens home – leave them for others to enjoy.)

From the elegant line of sandy beach at Waimarama and its prosperous beach community it's straight into boulder-bashing at the first headland. As a useful rule of thumb, if you can get round this headland easily you should have time to get to the concretions and back. Bare Island (Motukura) lives up to its name, though when Captain Cook passed it in 1769 it had a pa situated on it.

'At 2 p.m. passed by a Small but Pretty high white Island lying close to the Shore. On this Island we saw a good many Houses, Boats, and some people. We concluded that they must be fishers, because the Island was quite barren...'

There are broad boulder beaches at Te Puku Point that stretch all the way to Te Wainohu. Part of the cliff has collapsed just before Te Wainohu and you could escape up here to the pine plantation on the cliff edge.

Different rock styles abound, though you might have to get down on your knees to appreciate the variety. There are 'pencil holder' types, with holes drilled in on

115

CONCRETIONS

Concretions are hard round rocks that range from the size from cannonballs to the size of small cars. Although remarkable to us, they are all formed in a natural way, as described in *Reading the Rocks* by Lloyd Homer and Phil Moore:

'Concretions begin to grow in sediments soon after they are deposited on the sea floor by the precipitation of calcium carbonate (or lime) around a nucleus such as shell or a piece of wood. Since they are harder than the surrounding rock they commonly contain well-preserved fossils.'

The Waimarama boulders are huge but there are many smaller concretions on Red Island, further along the coast. Probably the most famous concretions in New Zealand are at Moeraki beach in the South Island near Dunedin.

every side, and 'sandwich' rocks, made up of neatly layered strata of differing colours. Some boulders are flecked with white splodges, as if some mad painter had splattered each one; others have swirls and spirals locked in them. There are also quite a lot of delicately segmented rocks, complete with barnacles mimicking the rock patterns.

Around the corner at Te Wainohu Point there is a fine view of the gracious Cray Bay, and in the distance the dusty brown colours of Red Island or Karamea. But the foreground is littered with large concretions, which have all tumbled out of an eroding clay cliff and settled into the tidal pools. Some are the size of a Fiat Bambina; others like the roundshot they used in canons in Captain Cook's day.

It is not far to Cray Bay, which is being maintained as a non-commercial fishing area for crayfish. The beach is a grand place for a picnic.

Red Island is another 2km of boulder-hopping away, and probably too far for most walkers. The fit ones will find a shattered volcanic island, connected at low tide by a sandy strip and composed of many different-coloured rocks and strata. In low light the rocks can be illuminated with a strange intensity.

BLOWHARD BUSH

Features
Podocarp forest, bush birds, limestone passages, kanuka and pumice ridge.

How to get there
From Napier or Hastings take the Napier-Taihape Road inland some 60km, and turn right onto Lawrence Road 1km to the signposted carpark. The main information board is about 2 minutes' walk in from the carpark.

Walking time
Full circuit (Tui Track/Kaweka lookout / Lowry Lodge/Tui Track) 2-3 hours.

Limestone overhangs and cave walk 30 minutes return.

Note: There is a confusing complexity of tracks within this small reserve, with an odd assemblage of signposting, as varied as the trees. The bush is open and there are several false trails. Children should not be left to wander on their own, and adults without a map might get fairly baffled themselves. The map in this book should not be taken as definitive as the track layout may change, so please study the main information signboard carefully.

From the Napier-Taihape road the Blowhard Bush reserve looks distinctly undistinguished, almost surrounded by forestry roads and dusted white by the lumbering logging trucks – but therein lies a secret: a limestone labyrinth of passages and fissures covered with dense podocarp forest. Tracks twist in quirky directions among the moss grottos of rock overhangs and holes, with vines and ferns that dangle over your head and lend an air of obscurity and charm to the bush. Children will think there are trolls about; adults will find it all rather odd.

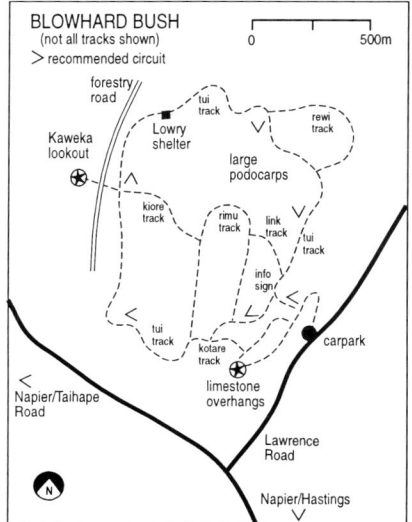

From the carpark it takes a few minutes along the track and a footbridge over the Otakarara Stream to the main information signboard. If you don't have a pamphlet map, study the map carefully.

You might want to walk the short Troglodyte Track circuit first as a separate side-trip. It takes only 20 minutes return and wanders about various limestone overhangs, beech forest and a small natural bridge. Follow the markers.

The main Tui Track circuit starts from the signboard and climbs slowly past large blocks of Waitotara-like limestone, arranged in a rather uncanny grid-like pattern. The air is dank and medieval.

Roots scramble up the smooth limestone in desperate attitudes and stone alleyways run off in all directions. The temptation to wander down them will be strong but please keep to the marked trails, as it reduces the damage to the bush.

The Tui Track passes several track junctions and gradually leaves the podocarp-hardwood forest, entering a band of kanuka forest, regenerating from previous burn-offs. Silver-eyes, robins, bellbirds, tomtits and whiteheads are all fairly vocal.

After some grassy clearings the track climbs into open pumice country that is being rapidly taken over by the poisonous native tutu. A side-track (well worth taking) crosses the firebreak road and goes to the Kaweka Lookout, where there is a fine prospect of the Kaweka Ranges and the massive pine plantation plateaus that surround this bushy enclave.

Back on the main circuit the track drops down through more open kanuka country to the Lowry Lodge shelter, then back into podocarp forest again and the limestone maze. You can't help but feel you are among the ruins of some ancient city, and indeed for a short time last century a Maori family lived in one of the overhanging rock shelters.

The track drops into an area of impressive podocarps – matai, rimu, totara all grow to some splendid heights here. After more track junctions the Tui Track drops down to the Otakarara Stream near some sinkholes and at last swallows its own tail right by the map signboard.

SUNRISE HUT

Features

Beech forest and bush hut, rocky lookout and alpine hut.

How to get there

From Hastings, drive via Flaxmere or Bridge Pa to Highway 50, and follow this some 50km to Tikokino. From Tikokino, take the Wakarara road 18km to the junction with the North Block Road, then follow this road 7km to the Triplex carpark, with several farm gates to open and close.

Walking time

Triplex Hut return 20 minutes.
Swamp Track circuit 1 hour.
Sunrise Hut return 4-5 hours.

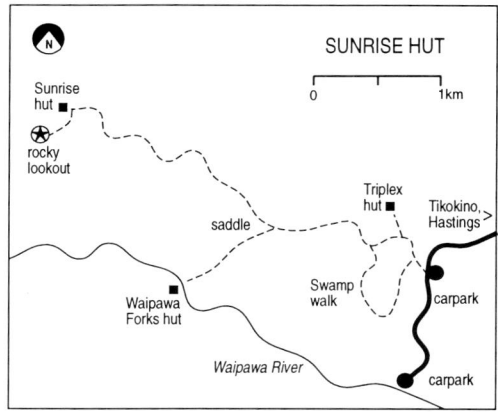

The track to Sunrise Hut is one of the most accessible trips to the tops on the western side of the Ruahine Range. A well-maintained 'garden path' zig-zags up through some splendid mature forest to a sunny hut beside a small tarn. The rocky lookout nearby provides a panorama of Hawke's Bay and the Wairarapa.

From the carpark a vehicle track winds around the hillside some 10 minutes' walk (past the Swamp Track junction) to the start of the Sunrise Track. A few minutes further the vehicle track reaches Triplex Hut, a 12-16 person hut, still in reasonable condition. Good camping in the grassy glade.

The Sunrise Track climbs slowly up through impressive red beech forest with occasional podocarps such as rimu and kahikatea poking through. Deep beds of crown fern on the forest floor soothe the scene. Bush birds are active and bellbirds and tomtits are curious enough to come and have a look at you. Parakeets can often be heard chattering in the canopy, though you rarely see them.

After passing the other end of the Swamp Track the main trail climbs up to a small saddle, where a side-track drops down to the Waipawa River and Waipawa Forks Hut. For the fit who don't mind getting their feet wet, this provides an alternative route out down the river to the Waipawa River carpark.

Mountain beech gradually replaces the red beech as the track climbs and you get glimpses of the ranges. Even so, Sunrise Hut comes as a surprise as you pop out of the bush into 'buttercup hollow' (the buttercups have gone, unfortunately), where the hut stands beside a small tarn. The hut takes about 8-10 people, and has gas cookers and a gas heater. The mountain beech has been forced into a crouch by the fearsome wind.

It's only a few minutes' scramble up to the obvious rocky lookout, where you get a great prospect of mountains, from Waipawa Saddle over the tortured scree ridges of Te Atuaoparapara (1687 metres) and round to Armstrong Saddle. The latter got its name from Hamish Armstrong who crashed a light plane here in 1935 and whose body was never found, except for a shirt with the trademark Triplex. In another version of the story the shirt was marked with three Xs.

Swamp Track

It seems somewhat perverse to call this a swamp track when there's precious little swamp to be seen. However, this is an excellent lowland walk, recently upgraded and suitable for sofa slugs. Amidst the moss carpet here are plenty of kahikatea, miro and rimu to get excited about.

BEECH FOREST

Beech (or birch, as the settlers knew it) is the most widespread and successful tree species in New Zealand. Beech forest prevails almost from Auckland to Southland, with only Northland and Stewart Island exempt from its advances. Unlike podocarps, which rely on bird dispersal, beech seeds are spread by wind so the forest expands more slowly but predictably.

There are four beech species in New Zealand. Red beech is a handsome tree and likes fertile lowland areas and mountain mid-slopes. It has the largest leaves, grows the tallest and is spread from East Cape to Southland. The 'red' colour can refer either to the bark, the wood or the leaves in winter.

Hard beech is very similar to red, and only botanists can really distinguish the two. As the name suggests, its timber is the most durable of the beeches and was once put to uses that ranged from railway sleepers to weatherboards. The silica in the wood blunted saws and chisels so it was never popular with wood-turners.

Silver beech (tawhai) is the most widespread and generally likes drier or higher slopes. It has a specialised parasitic fungus in the shape of a 'honeycomb' ball.

Mountain beech grows at the highest altitudes and has the smallest leaves, which have a distinct pointy end or 'peak' to them. Black beech is a variety of mountain beech.

Elephant weevil on silver beech

WAIRARAPA

CASTLE POINT

Features
Sea cliffs and rock formations, sandy bays, lighthouse lookout.

How to get there
From Masterton take the signposted and sealed Castle Point road about 50km to the coastal settlement.

Walking time
Lighthouse lookout return 30 minutes. Cave return 20 minutes. Castle Cliff return 2 hours, Christmas Bay return 2-3 hours.

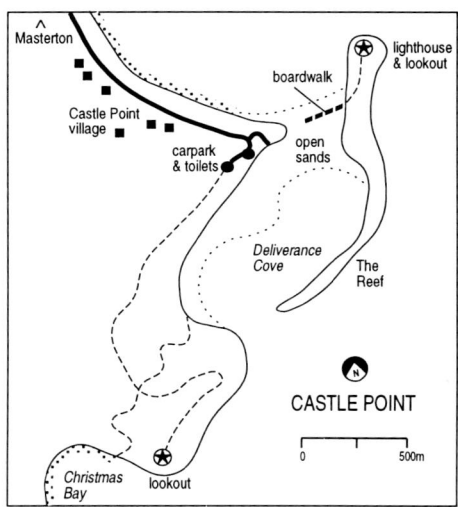

Few coastal villages have such a dramatic foreshore. An 'island' of battered rock encloses the soft sweep of Deliverance Cove and the lighthouse stands like a sentinel over the north end of the bay, while Castle Cliff rears up like a guard dog at the south end. Castle Point is famous for its notorious fishing reef, the fishing boats parked on the beach, and the annual horse race on the wide plain of sand.

The coastal settlement is a popular holiday resort in summer and on long weekends it can get busy, and getting a carpark becomes a competitive sport. From beside the toilets (and unfortunate concrete-block church) you can cross the beach sands and follow the raised boardwalk onto the rock island.

Occasionally seas break over the beach plain but for all intents and purposes the island is a permanent part of the mainland. The commercial fishers park their boats here, perched on trailers, and are backed out into Deliverance Cove by tractor in a noisy dawn parade.

A good track goes past the 20-metre lighthouse and a boardwalk carries on to the top part of the island. Stunning views. The boardwalk drops down to a sea-cliff terrace and you can make your own way around the battered and beautiful cliff platform back to the track. The agile can scramble up to the south high point of the island and overlook the reef. This curious feature extends a long articulated finger of smooth rock some 300 metres out towards Castle Rock cliff, so trapping and creating the lovely Deliverance Cove. The reef was shaped between two faultlines, each about two million years old.

No bones about it, this reef is dangerous. There are several warning signs at the base telling of the numerous drownings that have occurred when fishers have been caught by extra-large so-called rogue waves breaking over the reef. The waves are not 'rogue'; it is the fishermen pushing their luck a bit too far.

On a calm day with a light swell you walk out onto the reef in some sort of safety, but the rocks can still be slippery. Children should be watched carefully.

Admire the geological forces that created this strange limestone feature and the thickly crusted shellfish fossil that are embedded in the rock. Almost 70 species of fossils have been found here.

Seagulls haunt the bay, mainly the small and gregarious red-billed and the more solitary and larger black-backed gulls. The black-

RACHEL BARKER

Fisherfolk on the reef

KATIPO

While our near neighbour Australia revels in its deadly snakes, blood-sucking leeches, tiger ants and all manner of nasty things lurking in the undergrowth, New Zealand has only one poisonous denizen – the katipo spider. Unfortunately Australia has from time to time added to our short-list by slipping us the occasional red-back spider, altogether deadlier and more gregarious, and a close relative of the katipo. The red-back is now a permanent inhabitant.

The female katipo is about 1cm long, black with a red stripe down the middle of her back; the male is smaller, with a white abdomen marked with red and black. Only the female bites and in very rare cases her bite can be fatal. More usually it will cause localised pain and vomiting.

Katipo are notoriously shy – most people have never seen one, and even those people who look for them find them hard to locate. So it is disconcerting to realise that they are widespread and common, and any sandy beach environment like Castle Point will have plenty of katipo lurking under driftwood or clumps of marram grass. If you leave them alone, they will leave you alone.

Horse-riding on the beach

backs have a nesting colony on the sheer cliffs of Castle Rock. Reef herons, pipits and black shags all fossick about the rocks, and prefer to be left alone.

There is a good short walk to a sea cave from the beach (you need a low tide) but the main walk at Castle Point is up to Castle Rock. This can be made into a circuit, by following the beach sands across to the far end of Deliverance Cove and finding the well-worn trail up onto the saddle junction. People with vertigo might not want to carry on up to the high point.

The track sidles across the grassy face of the cliff and although the track is not steep the faces are. It can get wet and slippery after rain. There's a shrubby daisy here that is unique to Castle Point – *Brachyglottis compactus*. When the track reaches the ridge-edge it doubles back and wanders up to the top where there are excellent views along the Wairarapa coast. Take care on the descent and don't try to rush it.

At the saddle there is another worn trail that drops down to the delightful Christmas Bay, which is popular sandy bay and opens up the possibilities of exploring further along the wild coastline. The further you go the fewer people there are.

From the saddle there is a high-level track that circles around the top of the cliff edge, following the fenced farmland before descending easily through pine trees back to the carpark and the summer-time parade of people.

DONNELLY'S FLAT & GENTLE ANNIE

Features
Dense lowland bush, riverside flat and gorge, rocky lookout.

How to get there
From Masterton go south 5km on Highway 2, then turn right onto the Mount Holdsworth road (well signposted) for 15km

to the carpark. Ranger station, toilets, picnic area and the 30-person Holdsworth Lodge.

Walking time
Donnelly's Flat bush circuit 1 hour return. Gentle Annie track to rocky lookout 2-3 hours return. Atiwhakatu river gorge track 2-3 hours return.

Donnelly's Flat walk wanders about a romantic piece of forest with over-arching beech, straight-timbered podocarps (and some tortured rata), clingy epiphytes everywhere and a carpet of gorgeous kidney ferns. The river track sidles along beside the Atiwhakatu Stream and inspects a short, crisp gorge, and the longer walk up the Gentle Annie to the rocky lookout gains views over the Wairarapa and up to Mount

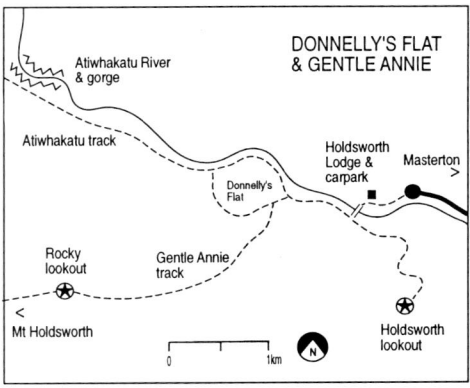

Holdsworth. The tracks are well graded, well signposted and there's something for everyone.

Donnelly's Flat Circuit
From the carpark the main track goes past Holdsworth Lodge and over the long fixed footbridge across the Atiwhakatu Stream. Just on the other side there is a side-track to the Holdsworth Lookout but the main trail runs around to the track junction with the Gentle Annie.

The forest is thick with splendid red beech, miro, matai and rimu, with astelia and makawe (hanging spleenwort) dangling off branches, lancewood filling in the understorey gaps and ferns crowding out the groundspace. Kidney fern is abundant. Sad and shrivelled up even after a few days' 'drought', but after rain it swells, and sunlight transforms the thin leaf structure into translucent greenstone.

Follow the Donnelly's Flat sign and quite quickly you enter a wide grassy clearing beside the Atiwhakatu. The silver pennants of toetoe edge the clearing, and the glossy poisonous green tutu along the riverbank is often spread by the blackbird. On the north side of the flat a short track goes into the bush to a splendid

Kidney fern

northern rata tree, with its aerial roots writhing up the main trunk – well worth the detour.

The flat is a good place to hear bush birds, even if you cannot see them. Bellbirds, blackbirds and tomtits are fairly loud, and fantails often burst out onto the clearing in pursuit of a frantic insect. Silver-eyes move in noisy, chirruppy groups. In the evening of course there are the plaintive cries of the morepork (ruru). The extinct huia was recorded in the Holdsworth area as late as 1903.

The track goes back into bush, passes the Atiwhakatu river junction and turns inland through mature and gloomy forest. Kahikatea have broad buttresses to give them some sort of stability on the boggy ground, and the fiercely competitive kidney fern tries to block out other fern rivals by densely covering the ground.

The loop track meets up with the Gentle Annie again and at this point you might be wondering, who was Donnelly anyway?

Atiwhakatu Stream Gorge
This well-graded track follows the Atiwhakatu Stream, climbing gently above the short gorge, with good river and forest views. You can go a long way up the valley but perhaps a good place to turn back is the Holdsworth Stream. There are plenty of places to get down to the pebbly Atiwhakatu and dabble a toe or two.

Gentle Annie and Rocky Lookout
'Gentle Annie' place names (and there are a lot of them in New Zealand) often refer to some difficult or steep hill. The goldminers in the 1860s brought out a popular sentimental Californian ballad that included the words 'shall we never see thee no more, gentle Annie'.

The original Gentle Annie walk in these parts was steep and rutted (you can still see parts of it) but has been superseded by this designer trail, which easily climbs up 300 metres or so to the Rocky Lookout. Fit people may race on to Pig Flat and Mountain House, even Mount Holdsworth, but the older, more cunning walker may find the sunbathed rocks of the lookout rather tempting. The views are also good.

Tom Donnelly might have passed this way; indeed he might even have sung the song about his gentle Annie. He was a South Island goldminer who, with his partner Fred Chapman, fossicked by the Atiwhakatu Stream in 1906, and their claim site was called Donnelly's Flat. But the prospector took on one hill too many for he died from exposure on the slopes of Mount Holdsworth a year later in 1907.

HONEYCOMB ROCK

Features
Geological formations, coastal scenery and islets, tidal platforms, fur seal colony.

How to get there
Take a road map. From Masterton take the Mania-Gladstone road towards Gladstone some 12km, turning off just before Gladstone onto the Tupurupuru-Te Wharau road to Te Wharau, another 20km. Here the seal ends and you follow the Flat Point road for 25km through the pine forests and down to the coast, turning south on the coastal road to Glenburn Station. All up, about 60km from Masterton.

The walk to Honeycomb Rock is well signposted just before Glenburn Station, and you must park here.

Walking time
4-5 hours return. Take your own drinking water. Walkway closed August-September. A low tide is not essential for this walk, but the beauty of the rock formations can be appreciated better if you have one.

Note: The walk is entirely on private land and special conditions apply. You must stick to the poled route (do not walk through the buildings at Glenburn Station), and you cannot visit the beaches without permission. In particular, any sort of surfcasting, shellfish gathering or diving is not permitted without the owner's consent. Leave gates as you find them and do not disturb the stock.

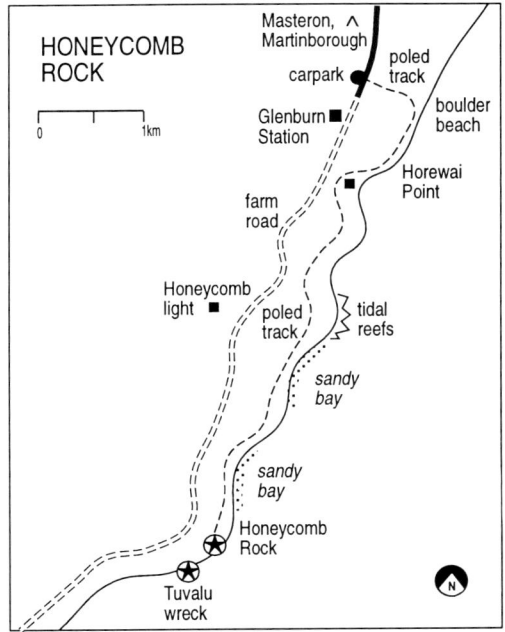

This is a walk for the keen – the walking is not hard but the driving is. Te Wharau is a long way from anywhere, a dusty, meandering gravel road into a beautiful but obscure part of the Wairarapa coast. Isolated baches are stuck out on the windy coastal plain; rock islets are dominated by shags. Get an early start and you will have a great day, walking along a foreshore littered with curious rock formations interrupted by sandy bays and reaching the weird and wonderful Honeycomb Rock. There are bound to be a few grouchy seals in the vicinity.

From the signpost follow the poles to the shoreline, and

Honeycomb Rock

then around the farm buildings (across a paddock at one point) until you are past the Glenburn Station. Basically the poles follow the grassy edge of the foreshore fairly closely, staying between the rocky coast and the vehicle track.

The shore rocks are bouldery at first but gradually you reach more intriguing rock formations as you wander along. There is a minor example of a honeycombed rock (with a hole) about halfway along the track, and you can see the main Honeycomb Rock in the distance. There are a couple of lovely sandy bays and large swathes of reef platforms as the tide goes out.

Honeycomb Rock is a cluster of larger rocks at the base of a headland, the surface of which has been 'eaten' (that seems the right word) into various peculiar shapes. The wreck of the *Tuvalu* is obvious just beyond the rock. This was a Fijian trading vessel that went aground here in 1967 on its maiden voyage.

Phil Moore and Lloyd Homer explain in *Reading the Rocks* how the cell-like weathering patterns were formed on Honeycomb Rock:

This formed primarily as a result of sea-spray soaking into the rock, saturating it with salt. As the rock dries out, salt crystals grow within the porous sandstone and in doing so, exert such pressure that they force individual sand grains apart. Then the wind takes over, rolling the loosened sand grains around in eddies until they form a shallow depression. Continued wetting and drying of the rock and grinding by wind-blown sand will eventually create a network of pits and hollows.'

Keep sniffing the air as you explore – in your distraction you might step on a seal. They don't like it.

RIMUTAKA INCLINE

Features
Bush regeneration, historic railway, train tunnels.

How to get there
From Wellington on Highway 2, just after Upper Hutt, there is a signposted turnoff to the Rimutaka Incline at Kaitoke, then it's 1km through old railway cuttings to the carpark and signboards. For the Wairarapa entrance drive to Featherston and take the Western Lake Road some 7km to a signposted side-road, where there is a carpark and signboard after 1km.

Walking time
A whole day should be allowed for the complete Incline walk – it's 16km: 4-6 hours one way right through. However for the less serious walker from the Upper Hutt side it's 3-4 hours return to the first tunnel and from the Wairarapa side it is also 3-4 hours return to the first tunnel. Take a torch.

Note: Walkers should note that this is a popular place for mountain bikers and although there is enough space for both users on the broad railway trail, some bikers really go for it.

The Rimutaka Incline was once the steepest railway in New Zealand, with 1-in-15 grade, which means for every 15 feet horizontally, the railway goes up 1 foot vertically. Modern railway inclines are usually around 1-in-90 to 1-in-200. The Otira tunnel at Arthur's Pass is considered very steep at 1-in-35.

Specially designed trains were needed to tackle the gradient on the Rimutaka railway. These fell engines had four wheels mounted horizontally underneath the train, which gripped on to a central raised-toothed rail. This cog and wheel set-up enabled the trains to get grip as they tortuously inched their way up the slope, and to brake on the way down.

The trains often had four locomotives spaced along the assembly and weighed over 200 tonnes in total. The maximum speed was 10 kilometres an hour going up, and 16 kilometres an hour going down. Often it was a lot slower –

slower in fact than most walkers would achieve today. The last remaining fell engine was restored and can be viewed in the Featherston museum.

Red admiral butterfly

The train incline ran from 1878 to 1955, when the Rimutaka railway tunnel was completed. The rails were ripped out, the township of Cross Creek closed, the glory days gone and the hills went to gorse.

The easy railway gradient has unintentionally made the incline popular with walkers and mountain bikers. Well-constructed tunnels, embankments and bridges have remained, and even the gorse has got its come-uppance.

The gorse sprang up after the early settlers and railway workers logged and burnt off the native timber. But allowing the gorse to remain meant that the native seed source still in the ground started up again, and thrived within the relative comfort zone of the gorse forest. Underneath the gorse it was windless, sheltered and frost free, so the native plants accelerated through the ageing gorse canopy.

The result is a regenerated native shrub landscape with gorse isolated in pockets and an encouraging flurry of native birds returning: fantails, tomtits bellbirds, wood pigeons and grey warblers as well as the ubiquitous chaffinch and blackbird. In time (a long time) this shrub forest will mature into tall native forest, and you can see the young rimu are there already, waiting in the wings, so to speak.

From the Wairarapa carpark the track avoids farmland and sidles around into the Cross Creek valley, crossing the stream onto the site of the old Cross Creek township. There is a shelter here, and excellent interpretation, with many historic photos and interesting anecdotes. It does seem astonishing that there was once a bustling township here, dominated by the smoke and timetables of the fell engines.

There is a side-track down to a well-sheltered campsite and a track fords Cross Creek and climbs to a lookout, and then drops down to meet the main track again.

From Cross Creek you are walking on the railway line proper, as it gradually snakes up the valley, climbing steadily before the first tunnel, Prices. You will need a torch for these well-constructed tunnels, some of which can get wet and even flooded after heavy rain.

The next tunnel is at Siberia and the line reaches the very long summit tunnel, which crosses the range and you pop out on the Upper Hutt side. It's easy walking with good views wandering past such pieces as Ladle Bend bridge, Pakuratahi bridge and the final tunnel at Pakuratahi. The line eases in grade somewhat and drops down past pine plantations to the Kaitoke carpark.

PUTANGIRUA PINNACLES

Features

Rock 'hoodoo' pinnacles and 'badlands erosion', seal colony, pillow lava.

How to get there

From Martinborough it is 35km past Pirinoa to the Te Kopi ranger station and carpark at the Pinnacles. Camping permitted.

Walking time

Putangirua Stream – Pinnacles 1 hour return. Putangirua Stream – Pinnacles – Loop Track – Bush Walk circuit 1-2 hours return. Pinnacles – Bush Walk – vehicle track – Te Kopi 3-4 hours return.

The Putangirua Pinnacles are a striking example of 'badlands' erosion, with stark gravel pillars poised somewhat perilously above your head. Stones crumble off creepily all the time, and you are aware that it is not a place to hang around in for long.

The Pinnacles are made up of greywacke gravels exposed by rain and floodwaters, an old alluvial fan deposit put down some seven or eight million years or so. Within these gravels are harder layers of rock that became 'caps', resisting the constant water erosion and creating individual 'hoodoo' pillars. The erosion processes started about 120,000 years ago and some pillars are thought to be 1000 years old.

The Pinnacles

The original bush in this area has been burnt off and logged, and the second-growth forest that is emerging is mainly rewarewa (New Zealand honeysuckle), hinau, titoki, lancewood and manuka. Beech forest lies on the upper ridges. Birds are the normal assortment of the more competitive native and introduced birds: chaffinches, thrushes, blackbirds, grey warblers, bellbirds, fantails and wood pigeons. The scarce New Zealand bush falcon is sometimes seen.

There are several short walk possibilities. The quickest way to the Pinnacles is up the streambed (crossing where necessary) into the heart of the amphitheatre of pinnacles.

A longer walk is when you come back out of the Pinnacles, you take the steep Loop Track up a spur from which you get excellent views down into the heart of the pinnacle formations before the track meets a top track called the Bush Walk, which can be followed back down to the carpark. Most families could handle this circuit.

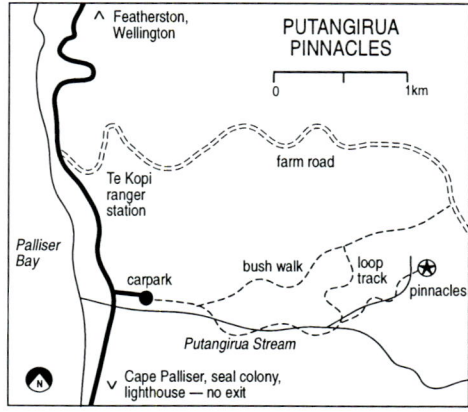

The last and longest walk is probably the best. First explore the Pinnacles, then take the Loop Track up to the Bush Walk and follow along this pleasant ridge trail until it meets an old vehicle track on the ridge-line. This road winds back through the beech forest, then over open farmland down to the Te Kopi ranger station. Superb views of Palliser Bay and the Kaikoura Mountains – this alone is worth the price of the petrol.

Cape Palliser

If you spend half a day at the Pinnacles you should spend the other half on the coast. The road hugs the shoreline all the way to the toothpaste-striped lighthouse with its remorseless 258 steps. It was built in 1897. There are many places to fossick on the beach reefs at Cape Palliser, with some good examples of pillow lava. Kupe's Sails are high slabs of sandstone rock and there are traces of 12th-century stone walls that date from early Maori occupation at the Stonewall or Waitetuna Stream.

The fur seal colony at Cape Palliser is the only known breeding colony in the North Island, but please, watch from a distance and never get between the seals and their escape route – the sea. As the colony expands you can expect to find dozing seals all along the coast.

TARANAKI

Shag

PARITUTU PLUG

Features
Volcanic outcrop, coastal views and offshore islands, marine reserve and beach, gull rookeries.

How to get there
From New Plymouth aim for the chimney of the power station, and follow the coast road to the carpark by the surf clubhouse. The start of the walk to Paritutu is not well signposted but obvious enough. Centennial Park is a short shift along the road with several carpark lookouts and access tracks down to the beach.

Walking time
Up Paritutu and back 20 minutes. Centennial Park beach walk 30 minutes return. At low to mid tide is a good time.

Paritutu, the Sugar Loaf Islands and Centennial Park are a backyard wilderness for New Plymouth residents, an excellent example of how with a little bit of care, humans and wild things can co-exist. There several short walk possibilities, and dozens of lookout points, from which you can admire the restless patterns of sea and surf around the islands.

PARITUTU PLUG
(most side-roads not shown)

Paritutu
In retrospect it was not the brightest idea to put a power station bang in the middle of New Plymouth's most scenic spot – but it ain't gonna be moved now. Indeed, some people have made a virtue of the massive chimney and think of it as a sister to Paritutu.

Paritutu is a spike of solid lava, pushed up out of an ancient volcano some 2 million years ago, and, with the Sugar Loafs, is the oldest volcanic remnant in Taranaki.

The track starts behind the old power station information building, with a warning sign beside the track. It climbs steeply up a well-eroded path to the quite roomy summit. It's not a difficult scramble if you are agile, but there are one or two exposed places with wires bolted in place. Remember it is always more difficult climbing *down*, so if you are having problems with your nerves going up, turn back. There are no fences on top so children should be closely supervised. The views are excellent.

Centennial Park and Beach

At low tide there is a good family beach walk of 30 minutes return from the surf lookout tower to the Paritutu cliffs. Seals occasionally haul ashore here and there should be terns and gulls hunting along the beach margins. Little blue penguins nest in some places along the beach, up in the flax and scrub, but these can usually be seen only in the morning as they leave, or late in the evening. If they see movement on the beach they often will not come ashore.

At low tide you can scramble onto Mataroa (Round Rock), which is an island popular with roosting sea birds, and the views are excellent on the top. There is an unofficial track to the top, which is the site of an old pa, and there are still food-storage pits visible.

An easy coast trail starts from the first carpark and winds through flax and scrub to the surf lookout tower, crosses the stream and continues for another 500 metres to end by the coast road. Good views.

SUGAR LOAF ISLANDS

There are numerous peaks and bumps around New Zealand called Sugar Loaf. It is an old-fashioned name for a large conical mass of hard refined sugar – it has nothing to do with bread. The term dates back to at least the 15th century ('a greate hyghe picke lyke a suger lofe'), when sugar was

RACHEL BARKER

sold in these conical blocks. In the Tudor period there was a fad for high pointed hats, immediately dubbed sugar-loaf hats.

Captain Cook named these distinctive islands in 1770. A marine reserve was created around the Sugar Loafs in 1991 and, fittingly, the rare Cook's scurvy grass (which is not a grass but a member of the cabbage family) is found on two islands.

There are at least 10 main islands with several smaller islets and rocks. The park has the northernmost breeding colony of fur seals in New Zealand and the area is brimming with wildlife. Of the thousands of sea birds that roost and breed on the islands, the likes of the red-billed gulls, stormy petrels, diving petrels, fluttering shearwaters, white-fronted terns and little blue penguins are common.

The undersea wildlife is equally abundant, with over 60 species of fish recorded, 60 types of sponge, abundant crayfish, and dolphins. Humpback whales and orca are seasonal visitors.

WHITE CLIFFS

Features
Sea cliffs, Maori pa, historic military tunnel, headlands and natural archway, the '600 steps'.

How to get there
From New Plymouth it is 36km north-east on Highway 3 to the turnoff into Pukearuhe Road and 11km to the end of this road. Carparking at the actual road-end is scant indeed, and may block access to the beach and to the farmland. It's not a bad idea to park in the historic reserve (signposted) and walk the last 500 metres down the road to where the track starts.

Walking time
White Cliffs Walkway is a long track that starts from Pukearuhe Pa and goes some 10km to Tongaporutu River. This walk description covers a shorter circuit along the beach to Wapingau Stream, up the stream track, and along the inland 'pipe' track back to the carpark. You definitely need a low tide to complete the circuit: the cliffs are steep with no escape routes. The inland track is closed for lambing between July and September.

3-4 hours circuit Waipingau Stream and 'pipe' track. 2 hours return to Waipingau Stream along the beach.

The road from Pukearuhe ends in a steep rock ramp that plunges straight onto the rollercoaster beach. It's quite a beginning. The sea cliffs look formidable, and it is easy to see why the pa at Pukearuhe was considered one of the finest fighting pas in the country.

Since the inland bush was dense and difficult for a large party to move through, the traditional trading and raiding path for Maori lay along the coastline. Pukearuhe blocked the way, and has had a long history of Maori warfare. In the Taranaki Wars the government forces occupied the pa and converted it to a redoubt in 1865, and some remains of the blockhouse can be seen. The memorial in the historic reserve is to the murdered missionary John Whiteley.

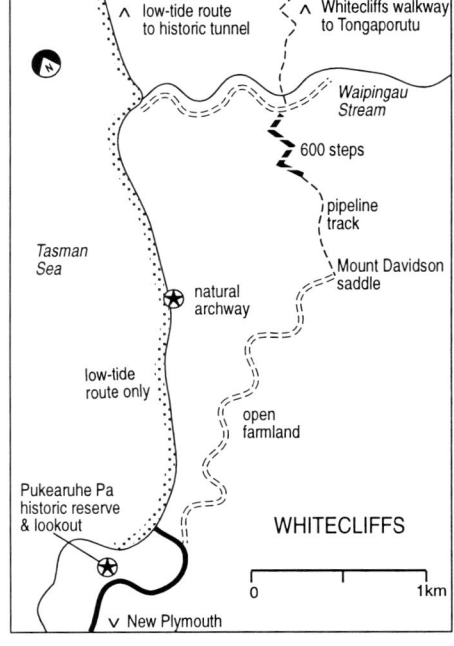

Today all the action is focused on the shore, and with a low tide it is a wonderful walk along the coast, past an attractive sea arch and tidal platforms to the

Cliff coastline

Waipingau Stream. After rain small 'donkey tail' waterfalls tumble over the crests of the sea cliffs.

As a side-trip, again with a low tide, it is a good jaunt along the shoreline to the historic tunnel. This was built by the military forces at Pukearuhe in the 1880s for better coastal access and subsequently utilised as a stock tunnel. Because of the erosion at the sea end, access to and through this tunnel is becoming problematic, and you should check the situation first with the Department of Conservation in New Plymouth.

The main track up Waipingau Stream is an old vehicle track and the valley is full of nikau palms and is also an important kiwi habitat. Tawa and rewarewa (New Zealand honeysuckle) are the main forest trees. At the track junction you are faced with the prospect of an enormous flight of steps (673 was one count!) up the spur to the Mount Davidson Saddle.

This track follows a public easement along the top of the Kapuni gas pipeline, the '8-inch', as opposed to the '30-inch' Maui gas pipeline. This network of pipes is a considerable engineering achievement and covers some sizeable distances. The Kapuni pipeline runs to Auckland and Wellington, the Maui goes to the Huntly power station, and a smaller pipe runs on to Whangarei. Another offshoot pipe supplies the Kinleith pulp mill.

After the sweat uphill, the views are excellent from the 250m-high Mt Davidson saddle, and it is easy walking down through the sheep paddocks and along the vehicle track (poled route) all the way back to the carpark. You can see Mount Taranaki on a clear day, and the sweep of coast where the land edge is crisply defined by the almost continuous barrier of sea cliffs.

THE PLATEAU

Features

Mountain views, leatherwood forest, alpine tussocks, rock formations.

How to get there

From Stratford take the road to Stratford Mountain House some 18km past the Stratford Lodge, and up the zig-zag to a huge skifield carpark simply called The Plateau. Lookout platform and toilets.

Walking time

To Tahurangi Lodge return 3-4 hours. To skifield public shelter return 1 hour. Obviously this is an alpine walk and you should pick your day. The walk described is suitable as a summer walk only.

The Plateau carpark, at an altitude of 1100 metres, is the highest carpark in Taranaki National Park, with outstanding views across the well-ordered plains to the squat volcanoes of Ruapehu and Ngauruhoe on the horizon. Behind is the trim Mount Taranaki one of the popular photographic symbols of New Zealand.

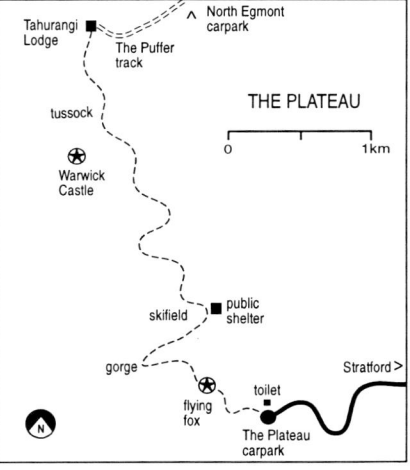

The first part of this track is also a service link to the skifield, which has no direct road access. The angle is well graded and easy as you pass through a thick shrub belt of alpine leatherwood and koromiko. You often encounter thin mist up here, which makes the saturated leatherwood gleam.

After you pass the flying fox arrangement, where the skifield sends its supplies across the Manganui Gorge, the track angles into the narrow valley.

Signs warn against lingering in the gorge, mostly as a winter precaution against snow avalanches but you can also often get rock-fall. Quite frequently, and even late in the season, the gorge bed is full of old avalanche debris, and it can get quite exciting negotiating across the hard-packed snow. Usually there will be a well-worn line of footsteps to follow. A short sidling climb out of the gorge and you are at the skifield, and practically the first building is a large public shelter with toilets.

Skifields in summer always look depressing, with bits of rubbish emerging from the melting snow and the ski-tow pylons looking forlornly out of place.

The track crosses in front of the skifield buildings and across a mountain stream, sidling around small alpine gullies filled with buttercups and daisies in spring. Ngarara Bluff is a distinctive volcanic outcrop, and the shape suggests why the Maori named it 'reptile' or 'monster'. The track climbs steadily all the way to

LEATHERWOOD – TUPARE

Leatherwood is a plant with attitude. A gnarled, stout, leathery alpine shrub (sometimes called 'leatherleaf'), it enjoys a formidable reputation among trampers who have to battle through it. *Olearia colensoi* was named after William Colenso, and it is a type of tree daisy, usually found at an alpine level, just below the tussock-line. It seems to thrive in damp, misty, wet, cold places, which should tell you something about the climate at The Plateau carpark. It grows at sea level at Stewart Island and has small white flowers.

    Leatherwood extends from the East Cape south and can grow to a height of 3-4 metres in some areas, notably the Ruahine mountains, and forms a thick and splendid alpine forest. Unloved, but not unlovely.

Tahurangi Lodge, crossing several creeks (which may or may not have water in them, or old avalanche snow) and leaves behind the alpine shrubbery for an open landscape of tussocks.

    The views are marvellous, the gradient fairly gentle, and the track well poled as it snakes under the volcanic outcrop of Warwick Castle. There are several smaller rock bluffs and it is not long before the TV pylon and Tahurangi Lodge come round into view. There is a small unlocked emergency public shelter underneath the lodge.

    If you have arranged transport to pick you up from North Egmont carpark, you can go down 'The Puffer' vehicle track (servicing the TV tower), which takes about an hour. Otherwise, return to the Plateau carpark, and since the track is mostly downhill all the way it is an easy and amiable task.

DAWSON FALLS & WILKIES POOLS

Features
Waterfalls and cascades, mountain views, 'goblin' forest.

Visitor centre, public shelter, lookout platform, information boards, toilets. Tearooms at the lodge.

How to get there
From Stratford take the Opunake road some 12km, then turn right on to Manaia Road and drive 8km to the top carpark.

Walking time
Wilkies Pools circuit 1-2 hours.
Dawson Falls circuit 1-2 hours.

'I like to go tramping at Dawson Falls, the climate's superb and the scenery enthrals.' So goes the old tramping song, and it's partly true. These two short walks are perhaps the most attractive in Taranaki National Park, with plenty of lookouts to the mountain, and picnic spots beside the dashing streams. The forest is thickly crusted with lichens and mosses, giving the trees a shaggy, fairytale look, hence the local name 'goblin forest'.

Of course the songwriter must have been having a joke, because the reason behind the profusion of mosses is the constantly, wet climate. If sunlight is your thing you had better have a squiz at the mountain before you start. Many visitors find this 'cloud forest' satisfying and eerie in any weather, and more so when the thick mist turns every dangling lichen into a beard of matted diamonds.

Wilkies Pools

At the carpark or visitor centre study the map boards carefully, for there are numerous track options in this area and although the tracks are colour coded and well sign-posted, there is plenty of opportunity for confusion.

The Wilkies Pools track immediately plunges into the 'goblin forest' and winds up an easy spur. There's one good lookout towards Mount Taranaki. The track crosses the bubbling Kapuni Stream, and you *shouldn't* get wet feet if you jump in the right places. After heavy rain this crossing may be impassable or dangerous.

There is some agile boulder-hopping required now as the track goes alongside the stream and, after passing a track junction, arrives at Wilkies Pools themselves. They are a series of water-sculpted rock pools running in a turbulent little cascade, pretty and cold. A worn trail follows closely alongside the stream, and fit people can scramble up, but be careful, some of the rock gets greasy.

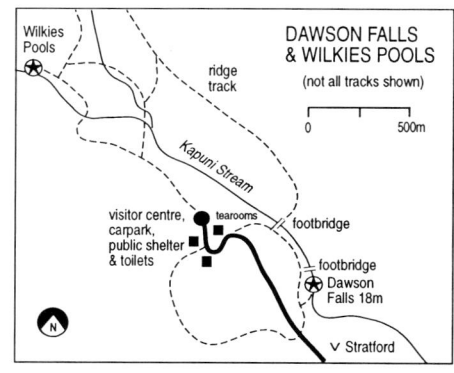

141

Ice beside the stream

Eventually this trail peters out in the upper Kapuni Stream, which has widened considerably into a gravel channel.

Return to the track junction and follow the new track briefly to a second track junction. Take this downstream option, which crosses over to a side-branch of the Kapuni, and very charming it is too. This track goes past several side-stream waterfalls, with mosses, alpine flowers and shrubs in healthy abundance.

Eventually a footbridge takes you back to the other side of the creek and onto the forest spur again and, and taking the downstream track junction, you should be back at the carpark in no time.

Dawson Falls

Dawson Falls is the scenic walk that most visitors inevitably do, and can be made into a circuit from the carpark. Find the right colour coding and walk back down the road a short distance to pick up the start of the track.

It passes one footbridge (worth a look) and drops down on a river terrace above Kapuni Stream. There's another footbridge shortly above the falls themselves, and just around from here an excellent lookout for those people who do not want to drop down to the base of the falls. Still, the signposted side-track is worth taking and the 18m-high falls look impressive from underneath. On a hot day you might even fancy a bracing shower.

The circuit track continues and crosses the road and, called the Kapuni Walk now, wanders back up to the public shelter and carpark.

142

WANGANUI & MANAWATU

RANGIWAHIA TOPS

Features
Bush track, mountain cedar forest, tussocks, alpine hut and views.

How to get there
A road map would be handy. The easiest route is probably via Highway 1 to Mangaweka township (the place with the café inside the aeroplane), then turn off towards Rangiwahia. It's about 15km from

Mangaweka to the turnoff onto Te Para Para Road, a further 4km to Renfrew Road, then 4km to the carpark. There are at least two gates to open and the road is steep towards the end.

Walking time
3-4 hours return to hut. Allow a further 1-2 hours to get to the main ridge and back.

At Rangiwahia you can see the great triptych of North Island volcanoes – Taranaki, Ruapehu and Ngauruhoe – and that's just from the carpark. 'Rangi' Hut is one of the most accessible alpine huts in the North Island, and few tracks can offer such a comfortable trip to the tops – it's two easy hours to the hut. The views start at the carpark but they get even better by the time you reach the bush-line.

By the way, it rains a lot in the Ruahines, up to 5000mm (that's five metres!) a year on the western side, and Rangi *is* on the western side. As many as 250 days a year it will be raining, so it pays to check the forecast, because it's hardly smart going to Rangi unless you are predicted to have a fine day.

From the carpark the track wanders up through some attractive rimu forest with pepper tree (horopito), rangiora and wineberry underneath. A grove of red beech and then an area of felled and ring-barked pine trees give the impression that some ardent conservationists have been very busy.

The bridge over the gorge is deliberately stylish and seems vaguely Chinese, balanced elegantly over the gorge. On the other side of the footbridge you enter mountain cedar forest, which is now becoming rare. Kaikawaka was known to early

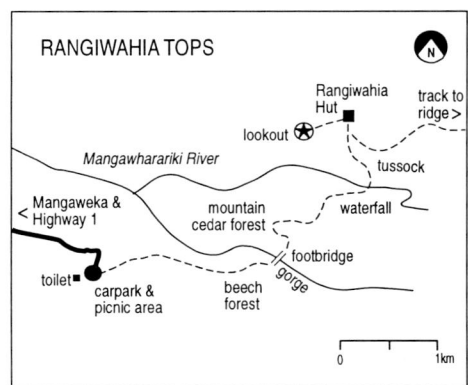

settlers as 'bucket-of-water tree' because it was notoriously hard to burn. It is a distinctive pyramid-like tree with a rich red trunk.

The track maintains its easy grade but zig-zags up through the sub-alpine leatherwood forest, which the Maori knew as tupare. Beyond a winsome waterfall you are on the tussock grasslands and there's the 12-bunk hut, with a red and white colour scheme that makes it appear oddly like a marae.

There's a veranda to eat lunch on and gawp at the views, and an even better lookout on the small hilltop beside the hut. Gas rings and gas heaters in the hut

It's certainly worth following the well-worn tussock track a wee way above the hut just to sample the expansive views of snowgrass, but the distance to the main ridge itself is deceptive. Mangahuia Peak on the ridge is 1580 metres high, but it's more than 3 kilometres to the summit from the hut.

You can find old pumice deposits throughout the Ruahine Range, and even on the tops as the old volcanic layers get exposed by the winds. You can't help but look back at Ruapehu and wonder whether the abdominal rumblings in 1995 and 1996 were just a case of indigestion or whether it really will blow.

Mountain cedar

SKIING THE HARD WAY

Rangiwahia Hut was originally a shepherd's shelter and a well-graded track must have been constructed to give access for the shepherd's pack-horses, and presumably to get the sheep up there. It could hardly have been successful pastoralism at these altitudes, and by the 1920s the hut had been taken over by hunters and a new breed of recreationist called trampers.

During the mid-1930s a group of local people began to explore the possibility of skiing at Rangi. The hut was smartened up and extended and a bulldozer brought up the rope-tow engine (an Indian motorcycle) and doubled as a snow groomer. By 1938 the Rangiwahia Ski Club was formed, the second ski club in New Zealand after Ruapehu. Fuel was carted in by shanks's pony.

The Second World War did no favours to club activities and although attempts were made to revive the club after the war, it gradually faded away. These days we like to drive to our skifields.

SNAPPER ROCK

Features

Coastal sands and sea cliffs, rock formations, tidal platforms, ventifacts.

How to get there

From Wanganui take Highway 3 about 15km to Kai Iwi, then turn off and continue another 5km-odd almost to Kai Iwi Beach settlement. Take the signposted Maxwell road about 4km to the Ototoka Beach road, then drive 4km on this road to the carpark on the cliff. Locally this is known as Maxwell's beach. Toilet.

Access to Wainui Beach is 30km from Wanganui on Highway 3 and 6km to the beach settlement and reserve.

Walking time

From Ototoka Beach to Wainui Beach is about 8km, 2-3 hours one way, and having transport arranged at the other end is probably the most attractive way to do this walk. From Wainui Beach, Snapper Rock return is another 2-3 hours.

It is important to aim for a *low tide* at Snapper Rock for this walk, particularly if you intend to go right through. The coastal cliffs are often not particularly steep and are interrupted by gullies and streams so there are escape routes if you misjudge the tides. At a pinch you can scramble along the cliff edge in a mixture of dunes, scrub and farmland.

From Wanganui to New Plymouth there is a continuous sweep of beach sands and sea cliffs. This exposed shoreline is a narrow margin of wilderness between the turbulent Tasman and the prim quilted farmland. This walk takes advantage of a less well-known stretch of coast that has retained some of its wild character, with interesting rock formations and large platforms of reef rocks at low tide.

Ototoka beach

The carpark at Ototoka sits on top of a cliff with fine views up and down the coast. You can see Wanganui city in the distance. A walking track crosses a smart bridge over a small waterfall then drops down beside the stream to the wide-open beach sands.

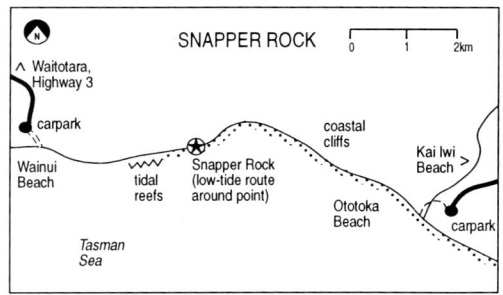

Scattered around here are numerous boulders made entirely of seashells. Indeed, the cement joining this conglomerate together is so thin in places you can almost break off chunks of shell in your hand.

As you walk west you quickly reach a headland where boulders have made a jumble of interesting shapes. Flax and marram grass secure the dune cliffs behind, and there are more intriguing rock boulders on the cliff margins. Ahead of you is the long sweep of Ototoka Beach, some 4km of open beach plain. Often the only inhabitant might be a lone patrolling black-backed gull.

There is no vehicle access at Ototoka Point, and the black rock pile at Snapper Rock prevents most vehicles from getting past, except at very low tide. As a consequence this beach is usually free from the pesky dune-buggies and trailbikes that roar along much of the western coast.

Snapper Rock itself (Nukumaru Rock) is a jumble of large flat rocks, which are a bit of a scramble to get over. At low tide there are various sand channels that enable you to walk around and underneath the rocks, but if the tide is wrong you may have to bash through the sand dunes. This area is popular with fishers, hence the name.

Around the Snapper Rock there are extensive reef platforms, intersected with placid tide pools and seaweed-clotted channels. The evening light infuses the intricate pattern of sand and rock with a wealth of warmth and detail.

It's 2km around several subtle headlands to Wainui Beach, which has a recreational reserve on the foreshore and a large carpark and picnic area.

VENTIFACTS

There's a large sign at Wainui Beach stating that the gathering of ventifacts is illegal. What, you might well ask, are ventifacts?

They are wind-sculptured stones, worn into shapes variously described as 'triangles', 'brazil nuts' and 'chinese hats'. Ventifact is a latin word meaning wind-made, and on this coast they have resulted from the stones of older beaches becoming exposed as the top layers of geologically young sand are blown away and 'sand-blasted' against the resisting pebbles.

Ventifacts are found all over New Zealand but particularly in more exposed beaches or plains, such as Awarua Bay at Invercargill, loess deposits in South Canterbury, or on the high plateaus of Central Otago such as Poolburn.

LAKE PAPAITONGA
& MANAWATU ESTUARY

Features
Bush lake and birds, estuary and saltmarsh, spoonbills, sand dunes, pingao.

How to get there
Lake Papaitonga is signposted from Highway 1 about 5km south of Levin. There's a small carpark and information board at the end of Buller Road.

Manawatu Estuary is 8km from Foxton at Foxton Beach. There are various access points. Just in front of the motorcamp at Foxton Beach a road swings out to the sand flats beside the river. Often these are firm and you can drive 500m further along the river to where the sand dunes are. However, you drive on these sand flats *at your own risk*. Many fishers with 4WDs drive right out to the river spit.

Walking time
Lake Papaitonga 30-40 minutes return.
Manawatu Estuary beach and rivermouth 1-2 hours return.
Sunset Walk 1 hour return.

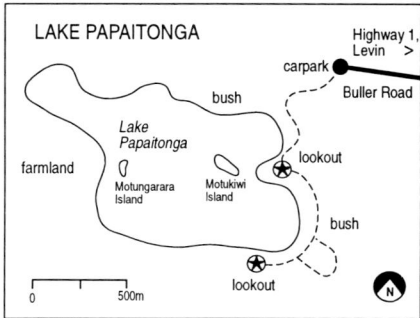

Lake Papaitonga

Lake Papaitonga and the Manawatu estuary are 18km apart as the tui flies, so linking these two walks together may seem odd. But they share a common legacy.

Most of the Horowhenua plain has been drastically changed from its pre-European days – the forests all logged, much of the original wetlands drained – and these two small areas are tiny remnants of what was once a glorious and wild lowland landscape.

It was perhaps inevitable. The lowlands were rich and fertile and the early settlers needed farmland, but the success of their bush clearance is staggering. Not just in Horowhenua, but all around New Zealand (with the notable exception of the West Coast of the South Island) the settlers turned dense lowland kahikatea forest into profitable farmland in less than 100 years.

One can wish at times that they had not been so successful, or that they made some more effort to protect something of the unusual natural heritage they found. One early conservationist was Sir Walter Buller, who bought Lake Papaitonga as a sort of personal estate and so managed to preserve it.

This short walk plunges into some lowland forest, full of birds and tall kahikatea, pukatea and tawa, with mahoe (whiteywood) and nikau palms occupying the mid-level spaces. Ferns and mosses fill up ground crannies and the flax, hebes and sedges fight it out on the water's margins. Cabbage trees mark the open spaces.

NIC BISHOP

Shoveller duck

Geoff Park in *Nga Uruora* tries to explain the magic:

'An intricate green kaleidoscope encloses you the moment you go under Papaitonga's trees. It's the same plain but the view suddenly drops from kilometres to metres. Instead of scanning far horizons, my eyes are led to mosses clinging to a supplejack vine. My senses adjust to quiet cool and closeness. Sunlight shafts through kohekohe, titoki and tawa, time-travellers from the ancient Gondwana tropics. Some sun ends on their highlighted leaves, some reaches the spread of nikau fronds or even the forest floor.'

It is a vibrant forest, the lake jammed with waterfowl, but from the two lookouts one can easily see that the density of bush is deceiving. Farmland lies on all sides, even

---

KARAKA

Karaka is a handsome, glossy-leaved coastal tree. In Maori mythology the seeds of the karaka tree were brought with them as a food source from Hawaiki, although the current northern limit of karaka today is at Raoul Island, in the Kermadecs. However, there's no denying karaka's importance. The fresh seed germinates quickly and many planted groves of the tree are found on the coast throughout New Zealand and in the Chathams, where it is called kopi.

As a food source the karaka fruit is not the most obvious. The seeds contain a highly poisonous substance called karakin, which causes paralysis, and they had to be cooked for several hours and steeped in a running stream for several days. Don't try this at home! The resulting product was non-poisonous, and is considered to taste rather like sweet chestnuts.

149

Wrybills

down to the head of the lake. The lake reserve is only 122 hectares but it is important for certain rare birds, such as the spotless crake and New Zealand dabchick, and the rare and beautiful *Powelliphanta* snails.

Manawatu Estuary

Estuaries have natural mechanisms such as flooding, storms and high tides that keep people at a distance. Yet even despite this volatility there are houses built optimistically all along the Manawatu River and saltmarsh, and the consequent noise, streetlights, cats and dogs all increase the fragility of the ecosystems here.

Yet despite the continual disturbance of humans over 70 species of birds have been recorded here. Some 38 species regularly use the estuary, and birds like the arctic waders such as godwits, lesser knots and bar-tailed knots come an awful long way just to do so. New Zealand migrants include South Island wrybills, oystercatchers and the snowy spoonbills. Permanently based local birds include banded dotterels, pied shags, white-faced herons, pied stilts and black-backed gulls.

There are two obvious short walks. The first is along the river edge out to the spit, then along the beach and back through the marram sand dunes (with occasional bursts of orange pingao, back to the carpark).

The second good access point for walkers is from the recreational and picnic reserve just above the motorcamp, and a signposted Sunset Walk follows a footpath in front of the houses around to the wharf and boat-ramps. As the name suggests, the evening light colours the saltmarsh in rare bands of red and gold and it is precisely this quiet time (if it is quiet) that the birds are active.

Looking at the cluster of fishermen (it is just about all men) and the cars, utes, three-wheelers, and four-wheel drives zooming along the beach sands, and trailbikes hooning in the sand dunes, it does seem amazing that the birds can take all this disturbance and still come back – perhaps they don't have any choice.

WELLINGTON

Damsel Fly

OTAKI FORKS

Features
River confluence and terraces, numerous
short walks, 1930s sawmilling sites and
boilers, camping and picnic areas, historic
bush hut.

How to get there
From Highway 1 just before Otaki
township and the Otaki River, turn onto the
Otaki Gorge Road and follow it some 19km
to Otaki Forks. The last 5km are narrow and
winding. Ranger station, picnic and
camping sites, information boards, toilets,
Parawai Lodge (24 bunks).

Walking time
There are many short walks around the
Forks, ranging from 10 minutes to 3 hours
return. For Fields Hut 4-5 hours return.

On a summer's day there is a nice easy feel to the Forks. The heat gets sequestered in between the hills and peaceful river sounds mingle with kids splashing boisterously in the clear pools. A bellbird call floats out across the open valley, and dragonflies seem to hover and stop for a breather on the somnolent air.

Just shows you how much can change. Between 1890 and 1940 the Otaki Forks was a place of ceaseless activity as a small back-blocks community established itself. The tall rimu and rata forest was logged out, the bush burnt over and farmland hacked out of the charcoaled soil. A tenuous, tough, self-reliant settlement struggled into life at Otaki Forks on the back of the sawmillers' success, and expanded as far as a schoolhouse, a post office and a manual telephone exchange.

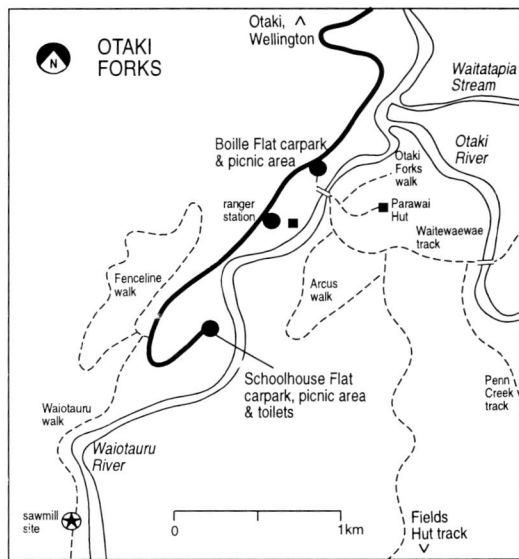

The First World War drew manpower from the area, and the Depression forced many to scrape a bare living from firewood cutting, batten splitting and possum trapping. The last sawmill closed in 1939 and the dreams went with it. *Life in the Gorge* by Les Marriot recounts some of the struggles and joys of that time.

The remains of this hard work are all around, though every year getting softer with regenerating bush: old boilers, log haulers, stone fences, tramways, chimney bricks, foundations and the spreading branches of a fig tree.

153

Toetoe

Short Walks at the Forks

Otaki Forks is the junction of the Otaki River and the Waiotauru River, with the Waitatapia Stream throwing in a good dose of liquid as well.

The walker is faced with many short walking options. From the picnic area at Boille Flat an old swing bridge crosses the Waiotauru River and there is plethora of choices here. A short track goes up onto a river terrace around five minutes to the Parawai Lodge, a tramping hut that, holds about 24 people. Sunny situation.

Another 20-minute side-track leads to a view of Otaki Forks themselves, passing old stone fences built during the Depression. A third track starts shortly along the Fields Track where there is a junction for the Arcus Loop Walk, a 50-minute poled return trail. Along the well-marked Fields Track is a junction for the Waitewaewae Track and Penn Creek. Slips further along the Penn Creek track have made access difficult and the track is not recommended.

The Waitewaewae Track continues and crosses the Otaki swingbridge and follows the tramline to Papa Creek and onto the remains of the old log-hauler. About 2-3 hours return. A good family trek without too much uphill.

From the Waiotauru campsite (or Schoolhouse Flat) there are two short walks. The Fenceline Loop (2 hours return) climbs through regenerating bush and across several small side-streams, while the Waiotauru Walk is a flat 40-minute return trip along the riverbank to the remains of the boiler and machinery from Seed and O'Brien's 1930s sawmill.

Field Hut and 'The Southern'

Field's Track (4-5 hours return) is on the start of the Southern Crossing tramping route, and climbs up past several farm terraces up an open bracken spur to the bush

154

edge. Great views from here. Older trampers will remember the notorious mud on this track, but the track is now well-graded, gravelled in many places and almost mud free, and follows up a fine forested spur to the historic Field Hut. There are many bush birds. Don't underestimate this climb – it is rises to 700-800 metres (2500 feet) and is suitable for fit walkers only.

Field Hut is the oldest tramping hut in New Zealand, and was the result of the efforts of the young Tararua Tramping Club. It was built in 1924, mostly by two experienced bushmen, J. H. Gibbs and J. Fisk. Their first job was to clear the track to Field so that the supplies and iron for the hut could be brought up by pack-horses. The timber for the hut was all felled from trees on site, and sawn on the spot in a pit-saw. The weather of course was poor, yet the hut was completed after only five months' work at a cost of £430.

Field's value lies mostly in its cultural and social history. As one of the first huts built specifically for tramping purposes, it marks the start of an important develop-ment in outdoor recreation in New Zealand. It was at the heart of a new 'tramping culture' that saw the development of such classic tramping challenges as Southern Crossing, which starts at Otaki Forks and runs over the tops to Kaitoke at Upper Hutt. Most of the Southern can be seen from any decent high-rise in Wellington.

Field Hut is an unusual two-storeyed hut and is still structurally sound, though some of the wood surfaces have endlessly overlapping initials carved into every niche. The place reeks of nostalgia, starlight and storms.

LANCEWOOD – HOROEKA

Horoeka is a most unusual plant because of its dramatic trans-formation. When a juvenile, it is a spindly stick with long downward serrated leaves, visually quite obvious and often an early starter in regenerating shrubland.

Then the tree does a masterly trick. It gets taller and thickens out, becomes bushy at the crown, the leaves shorten and fatten. Put the juvenile beside the adult and you would hardly pick they were the same tree.

KAPITI ISLAND

Features
Wildlife refuge, kaka, weka, takahe, kokako, saddlebacks, many bush birds, coastal scenery, historic hut, marine reserve.

How to get there
You'll need a boat and a permit. You can only visit the island via a licensed operator, and these can be contacted through the

Department of Conservation in Wellington. Kapiti Island is getting popular and the number of visitors is restricted, so you may have to book some months ahead.

Walking time
Trig Lookout and back 3 hours return. Okupe Lagoon 2 hours return. No fires, no smoking.

Kapiti looms large on the coastline north of Wellington. Steep-sided, dark-faced, with a line of breaking surf whitening the rocky edges, it hardly looks welcoming. Yet the island has been a refuge for Maori, a haven for sealers and whalers and latterly a wildlife reserve of outstanding importance for New Zealand.

The little spotted kiwi is extinct on the mainland and found only on Kapiti, and the island houses rare populations of tieke (saddleback), kokako, takahe, brown kiwi and stitchbird. The kaka are gregarious and memorable, and there is rich variety of bush birds and shore birds.

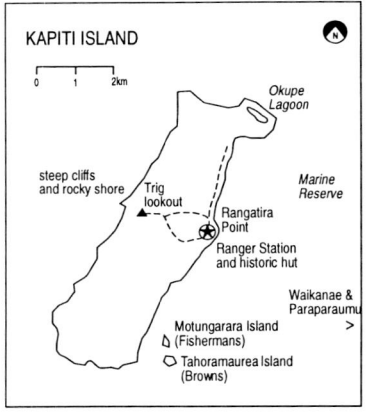

The history of Kapiti island would make a good novel. 'Ko te Waewae Kapiti Tara Raua Ko Rangitane' refers to the island as the meeting place between two relatives, Tara and Rangitane. Kapiti has been occupied sporadically and peacefully from 1200 by the Muaupoko and the later Ngai Kahungunu, until the Ngati Toa, led by the warrior chief Te Rauparaha, invaded in 1822.

Te Rauparaha then made Kapiti his base and fended off other tribal attacks. He seized the opportunities presented by the arrival of the Europeans and their new technology, swapped the shrunken heads of his rivals for European guns, and conducted raiding parties as far south as Christchurch. His activities became notorious and he was arrested in 1846, and died in 1849.

The whalers knew Kapiti as Entry Island (after Captain Cook's chart) and had up to seven shore-based whaling stations there. By the late 1840s the whales had mostly been hunted out, many of the Maori had shifted to the mainland and farmers had arrived. Despite three-quarters of Kapiti's virgin forest being destroyed, farming was always marginal. Sheep, cattle, goats, possums, pigs, cats and dogs were introduced, and of course both the Maori kiore and the European Norway rat made themselves at home. By the turn of the century Kapiti was a mess.

In 1897 Kapiti was made a reserve, and one of the first caretakers was Richard Henry, the famous custodian of Resolution Island. He had apparently failed to save the kakapo there and was disheartened about the difficulties of maintaining a nature reserve on Kapiti. Yet history will treat him more kindly and, ironically, if rats are eliminated from Kapiti then kakapo may well be imported to the island. Henry's house on Kapiti was the historic whare, which he repaired and lived in for 20 years and which may become a memorial to this pioneering conservationist.

There is a certain romance in being in a boat hauled by tractor across the beach and out into the rolling surf, but the short channel crossing can be stormy. Much of the sea channel between Waikanae and the island is now a marine reserve, which nicely complements Kapiti's conservation status. The boats land at Rangitira Point, where there is the DOC ranger station and the historic whare. It's a surprise to see a takahe nibbling the grass at the Point.

The DOC ranger will do an introductory talk on the importance of Kapiti as a wildlife reserve and the current restoration and conservation projects. Possums and goats have been eradicated from the island but the biggest effort in the next few years will be the attempted eradication of rats. Weka will have to be removed from the island first, because they are prone to eating the poisoned bait, and then re-stocked later. Kokako were introduced in 1995 and a continuing programme of restocking with rare native birds will be maintained until the numbers become self-perpetuating.

After the talk you are left to wander around, but there isn't a lot of choice of route since there are very few tracks. Most people look around Rangitira Point first, visit the historic whare, then take the Trig Track up the steep hillside and on to the Trig Lookout. You can then return via the Wilkinson Track to Rangitira Point.

Weka and takahe will be mooching around the point and at the old whare the North Island kaka will make a dramatic appearance. Although wild, these birds have

---

THE LAST RESORT

That's what the islands around New Zealand have been described as – the last resort: natural zoos with natural boundaries. As many New Zealand bird species come under pressure on the mainland, the islands off New Zealand are becoming the last resorts for their preservation. Kapiti Island (takahe, little spotted kiwi, kokako, saddlebacks), Little Barrier Island (kakapo) Codfish Island (kakapo), Pitt Island (black robins) Tiritiri-Matangi (takahe, saddlebacks): the list is endless.

The size of Kapiti Island makes it particularly significant – some 10km long and 2km wide, almost 2000 hectares in area. Its rugged terrain has held humans at bay, so only the coastal regions received much attention. Even so, some 70 per cent of Kapiti's bush was cleared at one time, and is only now slowly recovering.

Sadly, many bird species in New Zealand may in the future only be seen on island sanctuaries. In the battle between the aggressive introduced mammals and the native birds, the imports are still winning hands down.

A friendly kaka

become so friendly that they will crawl all over you for a handout – shoulders, arms, hands, head. The 'handout' normally takes the form of permitted dried fruit or cheese (no sweets or biscuits), and it is extraordinary to watch the kaka use their beaks and claws with great delicacy to sample the food. Like all parrots they are naturally inquisitive and they are not slow to try out a nose or two.

Saddlebacks may also come down, attracted by the fuss. These striking orange and black birds have a harsh 'machine-gun' rattle, and dance around the branches in an agitated display.

The Trig Track up to the lookout is steep, and joins Wilkinson Track near the top before reaching the lookout tower at Tuteremoana peak at 521 metres. The spectacular west coast is a fortress of cliffs and you are perched on its top battlement. An excellent place for lunch.

The original podocarps of matai, miro and rata have mostly gone and been replaced by a profusion of kohekohe, tawa and kanuka. Mahoe (whiteywood), lancewood and five-finger are common understorey shrubs, and karo has been introduced as a food source for many birds. Common bush birds on the island are bellbirds, whiteheads ('bush canaries'), New Zealand pigeons (kereru), tui, tomtits, long-tailed cuckoos, fantails, weka, silvereyes, kakariki (parakeets) and robins. Walk quietly and even sit awhile.

If you have time, Okupe Lagoon is worth visiting (two hours return) with several species of shag, as well as oystercatchers, gulls, paradise ducks, grey ducks, pied stilts and the elusive spotless crake.

On the bumpy boat trip back, the formidable bulk of Kapiti will look less sinister – more like a refuge than a prison.

PAUATAHANUI INLET

Features

Estuary and wading birds, saltmarsh, shag platform.

How to get there

From Wellington drive to Paremata and turn right to Pauatahunui as far as the road junction to Upper Hutt. Just beside the junction there's a signpost and a short side-road to a carpark. It's easy to miss it.

Walking time

30 minutes return to the shag platform. 1-2 hours to visit all the various bird hides. Take binoculars if you are serious about bird-watching.

Please keep to the tracks, and ensure that the shutters on the bird hides are replaced after use. Go slowly and carefully; if you arrive too quickly at a pond the birds will take fright.

On one of the estuary information boards the colourful fields of jointed rush are described as 'rushland'. Now surely that's an inspired name for Wellington.

The Pauatahanui inlet is in the tarmac grip of a ring of roads, bustling with car and lorry traffic, day and night. On the water, weekenders inspect all the margins of the estuary for fishing, boating and water-skiing, and that ingenious noxious mechanism, the wet bike, scatters a swathe of noise over the inlet. One wet biker can annoy several hundred quiet users – but then that's the idea, eh?

Even at night the estuary is not left entirely alone. The neon road lights cast an orange glare onto the waters, and streetlights string uncultured pearls up and down the hillsides. In the dark, still centre is the estuary and saltmarsh.

It's almost a dead cert that the first bird you will see in this reserve is a pukeko, scavenging among the tall grass and sedges beside the carpark. Always wary, never letting people get too close, it will quickly scuttle off.

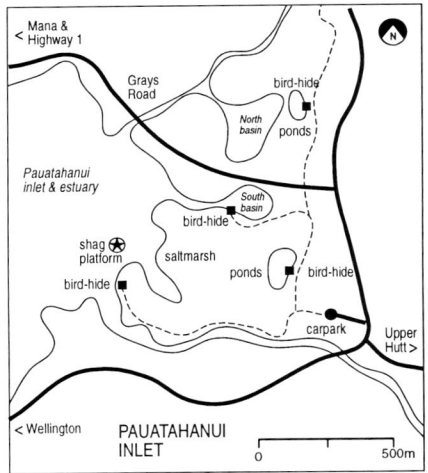

But another 47 species of birds have been identified in the inlet, most commonly the mallard, paradise shelduck, little and black shags, pied stilt, caspian tern, banded dotterel, white-faced heron, godwit, kingfisher, welcome swallow and harrier hawk.

There are several short tracks and boardwalks to four bird-hides, which give something of a bird's eye view of the estuary. The walk to the shag roost follows the Pauatahanui Stream, and often you will see black swans and kingfishers along here. Open the bird-hide shutters carefully, for on driftwood right beside the hide you can often see

PUKEKO

This is at once a familiar and exotic bird. It lives and thrives on the edges of human behaviour, dodges the cars (most times) and pokes its head out of raupo next door to the dairy. Stroppy and yet wary, it will quickly flap away, demonstrating one of the advantages it has over its close cousin, the rare and flightless takahe. Surprisingly the pukeko is found worldwide – on many South Pacific islands, in Australia, Africa, southern Asia, Spain and Portugal, Central America and Florida. Despite its laboured flight it is believed the pukeko flew in from Australia about 1000 years ago.

Technically it is a rail like the weka, likes wetlands and feeds on roots, seeds, grasses and occasional grubs. They live communally, females often sharing the same nest (a most unusual trait among birds), and both males and females help with raising the chicks. This egalitarianism seems to ensure highly successful breeding rates, for it is a poor piece of swamp that could not boast a few 'swamphen'.

a gaggle of shags: the shag platform is usually densely occupied, with sedate roosting shags who studiously ignore the mass of close neighbours.

The walk to the South Basin hide is well worthwhile, especially for the superb saltmarsh. Restless fields of jointed rush form a red-orange garden that in some lights become enriched with subtle and soft gold textures.

The track to the North Basin crosses Grays Road (watch it, the cars race down here), and you enter a mixed saltmarsh and freshwater ponds with flax, manuka and marsh ribbonwood. Further on a track is being extended through semi-shrubland of kanuka and manuka. This track (like the other estuary walks) has been developed by volunteers of the local Forest and Bird Society. They have to be congratulated for rescuing a marginal, unloved piece of saltmarsh – and not a dumped car body in sight.

MAKARA BEACH

Features
Headlands, rock pools and tidal platforms, Maori pa site, views of Cook Strait, historic military sites.

How to get there
From Wellington city drive through the suburb of Karori and take the road to Makara, some 16km in all. Toilets and café at carpark.

Walking time
Full coastal circuit 3-4 hours. Low tide not essential, but useful for fossicking in the rock pools. The headland part of the walk is closed for lambing from August to October.

Makara has a well-deserved reputation for being windy and wild. Your lungs will get a good workout, and it's not a place for those people who fear bad-hair days. The views along the stark grey coastline are uncompromising and the rock pools host subtle colours of life and death. The grunt up to the military fortifications brings worthwhile views of a South Island that looks unreasonably close – as if someone's moved it.

Follow the vehicle track around Makara Beach to Fisherman's Bay (Warehou), where a poled route heads up a gully and overlooks the faint terraces of a pa known as Te Upoko o Te Ika. Makara has been occupied by Maori for a long time – some of the umu (earth ovens) on the beach have been dated to 1070. Defensive ditches, post holes that supported the pallisade (which might have been 4-6 metres in height), and terraces can still be seen. Totara wood in the post holes has been dated to about 1640.

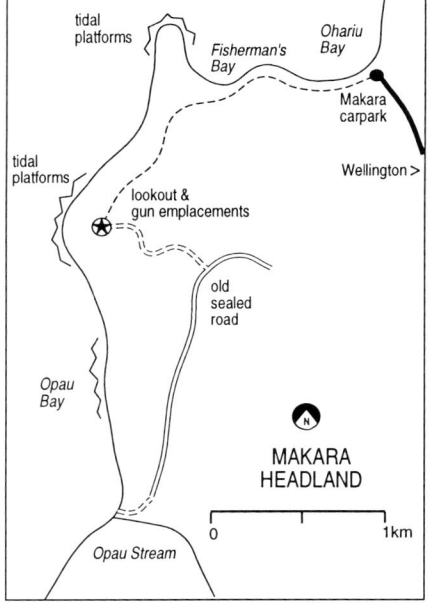

The views above the pa are good already, and by the time you've managed the steep grass spur up to the old military fortifications you will have reached the highest point on the track circuit – 201 metres.

The gaunt gun emplacements are empty of any intent now; indeed they never fired in rage. They were built hastily in 1942 as a consequence of the Japanese scare, but by 1944 were abandoned. There was a full barracks and quarters for the men.

Bull kelp

When they were not looking for the Japanese, the battalion must have enjoyed the stunning views of Kapiti Island, Mana Island, Cook Strait, Marlborough Sounds.

The poles turn uphill a bit and reach the top of an old sealed road, which was one of the access roads to the gun sites. It is easy walking down to Opau Bay, where you are faced with a boulder bash back to Makara. Just under the cliffs there is a well-worn trail that avoids the worst of the boulders and is easier walking. Once around Warehou Point you get back on to a good track again.

There is a mess of detritus on the coast. Driftwood tangled with old buoys, festoons of dry seaweed entwined with the remains of fishing nets. Often the rotting seaweed is darkened with sudden swarms of midges, and the vivid inner luminescence of a paua shell looks forlorn on the grey boulders. White-faced herons are common along the shoreline.

If it is blowing a southerly gale you will be glad to get around Warehou Point and a respite from the wind. There is something about beaches, boulders, sand and sea air that is peculiarly bracing – and knackering. An espresso is a good way to take the salt out of your mouth.

COOK STRAIT – RAUKAWA MOANA

It is not for nothing that we refer to 'desperate straits' or 'dire straits' when we see someone in difficulties. Sea-channels between two land masses are often turbulent and dodgy areas to navigate through. The English Channel, Foveaux Strait, the Straits of Gibraltar are all notorious 'squeezes'. For sailing ships Cook Strait was a nightmare. The currents are strong, accelerated by the close land masses, and large tides add a dangerous element. Cook Strait lies in a latitude where gales are common and winds rise in the confined area and can bounce off the hills with unnerving and unpredictable violence.

Add good doses of sea mist and shallow rock reefs and you can see why a certain cautious Yorkshireman in 1770 manoeuvred carefully in the unfamiliar passage. At his anchorage at Queen Charlotte Sound (named after the king's wife) he climbed a hill on Arapawa Island and was the first European to see through this stormy stretch of water to the Pacific – and we have called it Cook Strait ever since.

THE CATCHPOOL

Features
Bush walks and picnic areas, braided river valley and bach community.

How to get there
From Wainuiomata the Catchpool is 10km south on the coast road. Extensive carparking and picnic areas along the Catchpool Stream. Visitor centre, toilets, camping and information boards.

Walking time
Orongorongo Track to the Orongorongo River 3-4 hours return. There are many shorter tracks – see signboards. The Catchpool reserve gates are locked at dusk.

Note: the Orongorongo Track used to be commonly known as the Five Mile, but this name has been transferred to another loop track in the Catchpool reserve. The actual distance to the Orongorongo River is about 5km. It is the Catchpool Stream that the Orongorongo track follows closely, and the name comes from an early settler, Edward Catchpool.

One early pamphlet laconically described the bush along the Orongorongo track as 'mixed forest'. Mixed indeed! Rimu, totara, kahikatea, nikau palm, miro, tawa, hinau, rewarewa and beech: the whole works in a thoroughly jumbled and satisfying hardwood and podocarp forest. At the end of the track are the wide braided gravels of the Orongorongo River, with its discreet and quirky collection of private baches.

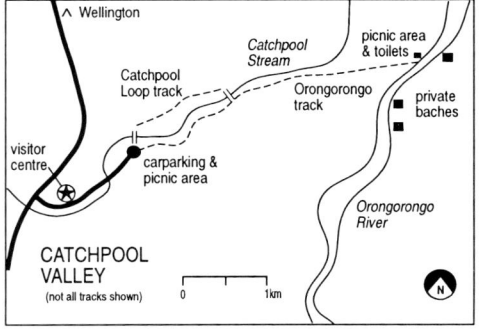

The Catchpool is a pretty valley, with extensive picnic, parking, camping and barbecue areas. On a hot summer Sunday the place is alive with day-trippers cooling off in the crystal-sharp waters of the Catchpool Stream, though the water scarcely rises above chilly. The information centre has some interesting history and sells campsite tickets and some basic food items – like chocolate bars.

At the carpark at the end of the reserve road there is a large map signboard and the Orongorongo Track climbs easily through pine trees before dropping down into native bush. The side-creeks are well bridged and after 30 minutes or so there is a side-track called the Catchpool Loop that takes you back to the carpark. This is a good short walk for those who do not want to do the whole trail.

The bush is dense, with every bit of ground space filled up with ferns such as the crown fern (piupiu), hound's tongue (kowaewao) and starfish fern (kiwakiwa).

THE BACH IN THE BUSH

There has been four-wheel-drive access up the Orongorongo River for many years via the coast at Baring Head, which explains the 50 or so private baches tucked away in the bush. Some are barely more than tin sheds, others are palatial, many are eccentric. One has a telephone box toilet. The baches hark back to a do-it-yourself era when all a Kiwi family aspired to was a bach by the beach, or in the bush. Plenty of fresh air, slops out the door, and possums in the dunny. There must be hundreds of these small communities around New Zealand, and every road-end that peters out on a sandy bay has a huddle of corrugated iron cottages, leaning into the wind, blistered by sun.

But times change and most remote locations have become easily accessible, with fast sealed roads and new cars. We are more mobile and less patient. The family can get to the bach and be back in town in a comfortable day, and most baches stand empty for 11 months of the year. The effort of maintenance has rather lost its charm – we'd rather go to the Gold Coast or Fiji.

The Department of Conservation has a policy of gradually removing the baches in the Orongorongo Valley once the owner has died (the baches are on public conservation land) and slowly this era is coming to an end. All that will remain are fading black and white photos of long summers gone.

If you want to hear and see bush birds, walk slowly and quietly, on your own if you can, or in small groups. Sit still for a while and the birds will get on with feeding. As the old saying goes, 'birds of a feather flock together', and one species of bird will be feeding in association with another species. Not only do these loose bird groups use each other to hunt out where the good food is, but they rely on each other for safety signals. Larger, noiser birds may flush out insects that other birds can take advantage of.

In the North Island whiteheads often lead food 'hunts', with fantails and brown creepers joining in. In the South Island yellowheads and parakeets traditionally and noisily forage ahead, followed by a train of grey warblers, brown creepers and fantails. So you get this odd effect in New Zealand bush of 'dead zones' where there seem to be no birds and 'live zones' where there will suddenly be several species feeding and calling to each other all at once, as they move through the forest.

Gradually the well-graded path reaches the head of the valley (passes the Cattle Ridge Track) and crosses a low, almost indistinguishable saddle. It slopes past drops past the Mckerrow Track junction and descends sharply to the attractive arched bridge over the Turere Stream. There's a dark brown swimming hole here, with toilets and a picnic area a minute or so further, out on the wide Orongorongo riverbed.

Features

Shoreline walk, views of Cook Strait and Kaikoura mountains, coastal freshwater lakes, sea birds, historic lighthouse.

How to get there

From Wellington or Lower Hutt take the Eastbourne Road to the carpark and information signs right at the end of the road by the locked gate. During the summer a mountain bike operator sets up shop in the carpark, and since the 'track' is mostly a vehicle road, this is an option worth considering.

Walking time

4-5 hours return to the lighthouse. Although it's easy walking, it's further to the lighthouse than you might think, so keep an eye on the time. Every step forward has to be retraced unless you can hitch a ride on a mountain bike.

Wellington's Latin motto states it simply enough: *suprema in situ* or in Kiwi idiom, 'a neat spot'. Nothing can match the capital on a fine day, although most people want to leave town when the southerly arrives.

The harbour of Poneke is one of the most sheltered in New Zealand, and yet at times one of the wildest. The famous winds that come out of Cook Strait give rise to a good many of the jokes about 'windy Wellington', and also some of its tragedies. From the Pencarrow walk you are only 500 metres away from Barretts Reef, which was the site of the sinking of the ferry *Wahine* in 1968, which drowned 51 people.

The Cook Strait ferries are a feature of this walk, as they (not surprisingly) tend to steer clear of Barretts Reef and come close to Pencarrow Head. The new fast ferries whisk in and out like vast metallic terns.

From the carpark at Point Arthur the vehicle track winds around numerous small stony bays and as you leave behind the more laid-back picnickers, each turn in the track reveals another angle on Wellington's hills. Rock outcrops protrude from the pebbly beaches and black-backed gulls patrol the shoreline. Pied and black shags roost along the coast and white-faced herons are often on the rock reefs at low tide. Little blue penguins come ashore at dusk.

Just before the working automated lighthouse on the shoreline, obvious side track climbs up to the historic lighthouse. This was built in 1859, the first lighthouse in New Zealand, and has the unusual distinction of being 'manned' at one time by New Zealand's only female lighthouse keeper, Mary Jane Bennett. She lit the light for the first time on 1 January 1859 and worked at the light with her five young children until about 1865. She was assisted by a junior keeper from 1860. The light was finally closed in 1935.

It's well worthwhile to continue beyond the lighthouse and up onto the grassy peak, with excellent views over the first coastal lake, Kohanga-piripiri, and towards Cook Strait and the Kaikoura mountains. A vehicle track leads down to the brink of the lake, which supports a variety of waterfowl such as pukeko, oyster-catchers and pied stilts. Pukeko and spotless crakes breed here. It's not a long extra walk along to the next lake, Kohangatera, and both lakes have important wetlands and are relatively undisturbed.

On a fine evening the setting sun illuminates the cliffs and placid Wellington Harbour, and provide some compensation for the long trudge back.

NIC BISHOP

Whistling frog, fresh water lake shore

NOTES

NOTES